MsP

DESIGN FOR LIVING

...[...] was to [...] and mistrustfully at some intense

[...]gant mystery — To keep the eyes so long on one thing was too [...]

I could come to any conclusion it occurred to me that my [...]

[...]tions of mine, would be mere futility. What did it matter w[...]

[...]ed? What did it matter who was manager? — "We will all b[...]

[...]t think a single one of them had any clear idea of time, a[...]

[...]have. They still belonged to the beginnings of time — had n[...]

[...] as it were), — legitimate self-defence. You can't breathe dead h[...]

[...], and at the same time keep your precarious grip on exist[...]

[...]ire itself, or made loops of it to snare the fishes with, I don[...]

[...]agent salary could be to them — Why in the name of all the gna[...]

[...]t go for us — they were thirty to five — and have a good tuck[...]

[...] think of it. They were big powerful men, with not much capacity [...]

[...]courage, with strength, even yet, though their skins were no lo[...]

[...]ger hard — Yes; I looked at them as you would on any human be[...]

[...]es, motives, capacities, weaknesses, when brought to the test of[...]

[...]bity. Restraint! What possible restraint? Was it superstition, [...]

[...]imitive honour? No fear can stand up to hunger, no patience ca[...]

[...]nd exist where hunger is; and as to superstition, beliefs, and wh[...]

[...]ve less than chaff in a breeze. Don't you know the devilry of [...]

[...]erating torment, its black thoughts, its sombre and brooding [...]

[...]all his inborn strength to fight hunger properly. It's really easier to fo[...]

[...]the perdition of one's soul — than this kind of prolonged hunger[...]

[...], too, had no earthly reason for any kind of scruple. Restra[...]

[...]ed restraint from a hyena [...]

DESIGN FOR LIVING

PAULA SHUTKEVER

DESIGNED BY WAYNE CAMPBELL

Part of the author's proceeds of this book are being donated to a charity chosen by the Manic Street Preachers' management company.

First published in Great Britain in 1996 by Virgin Books

332 Ladbroke Grove
London
W10 5AH

A catalogue record for this book is available from the British Library
ISBN 0 7535 0078 7

M S P

The band
that likes
to say

100% ARTIFICIAL INSINCERE HYPOCRITICAL GUARANTEE

MSP DESIGN FOR LIVING

ACKNOWLEDGEMENTS

SO I spent a sunny Sunday afternoon leafing through other pages of this kind, trying to work out another way of doing it. I was stumped and decided to go with the cryptic-message approach. Gratitude is too small a word to extend to those who have made my life so much easier in researching and writing this book. However, in no particular order, I'd like to express my thanks to:

Mal Peachey for the idea and choice of writer in the first place. Uncle Fred Dellar for giving me access-all-areas to 'Fred's Shed'. Louise Johncox and Mel Bradman for additional research. Damon 'Time for tea yet?' Wise, who encouraged me when others, who should have, didn't. Everyone at Hall Or Nothing – Caffy, Karen especially, and Terri, who I landed in a really difficult position by doing this (I hope it's everything I promised). Also, Lucy O'Brien, Patrick Humphries, Roy Carr, Ann Scanlon, Neil Perry and David Sinclair, who gave me sound advice, support and inspiration. Alan Lewis, for giving me my first job in music journalism (how about a pay rise?). For those who chose, with principle, to give additional information and did not want to be named, thank you; you know who you are. To all those journalists whose work I've utilised here, I am very grateful. To everyone who put up with my mood-swings during this project; my family, who brought me up to strive for integrity at all times and to believe that we should never forget our history. Also they haven't seen me for months (Audrey, Ralph, Leon, Claire, David, Bobby, Heather, Gary, Marnie, Avi, Erin, Zak and Max – thank you). Thanks to the residents of Number 20 (Maj for devoting so much of his time to reading material and talking endlessly about Apocalypse Now; Mandie for the healings, food and copious amounts of tea; and the beautiful Graham – you can stop screening the calls now). Also this is for Jack who provided the calming space in which to work – I am inspired daily by your love and exceptional courage. Thanks also to Karen Walter, Joe 'Fish-boy' Hickey, Sylvia Smith, for 24 wonderful years of friendship, Alex and Jo, Katya Rowledge, Juliet Eve, Glyn Busfield and Sue 'Auntie Dude' Castling, who (among many other wonderful things that she has done for me) took me to see the Manics at The Astoria at Christmas 1994. What a gig! What a hangover! The Tooting Trio of Helen 'Two-trees' Taylor, Wendy 'Soundgarden' Anderson and Moz-Cat – sorry for all my strange habits over the last three years. Josie Hartley and Martin Bailey for the love, humour and holiday I'm going to have with you after this has gone to press; Pete Avery, for just being Pete; the exceptionally dodgy Doug Lyon; and the very lovely Shaunie Phillips and family. For academic-type nonsense and friendship: Richard 'Completely hopeless' Woodcock and Dave Laing. Mark Ranaldi and Wayne Campbell – thank you for listening to me burble on for so long and making this look so wonderful. Also, dear Andy "This is our universe – big, isn't it?" Robson; you said I could do it – now, how about breakfast?

If I've missed anyone out, I'm sorry and thank you. There are, of course, two outstanding debts to pay.

The first is to the Manic Street Preachers themselves for being so inspiring and articulate: you are every music journalist's dream. This book was written with the word 'INTEGRITY' plastered over my Mac and your music on non-stop play. I hope you approve. The second is to the Manics' incredible fans. I hope this pulls together their history for you with quotes you wanted to read again, images you wanted to keep and some fresh parts, too. You are all amazing.

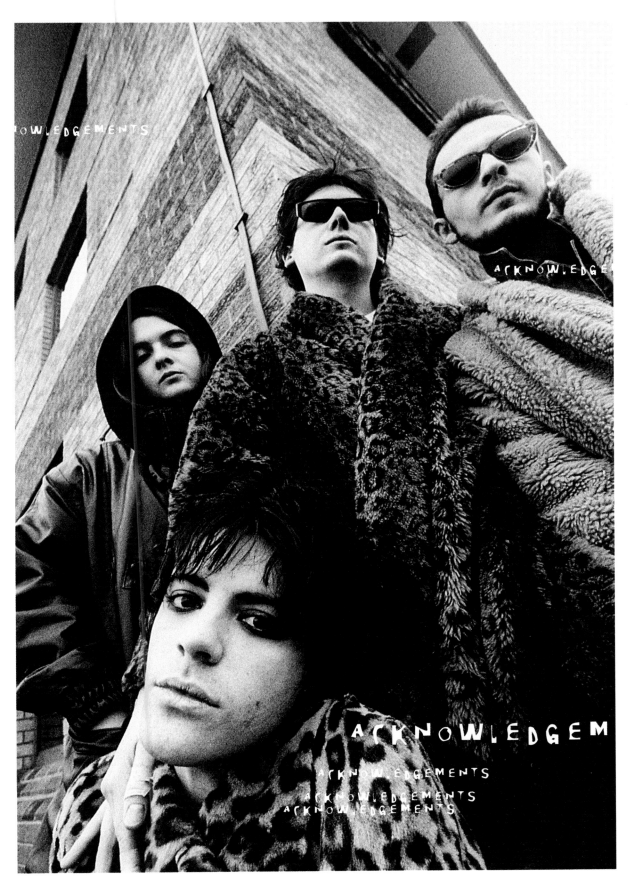

ACKNOWLEDGE

ACKNOWLEDGEM

ACKNOWLEDGEMENTS

ACKNOWLEDGEMENTS
ACKNOWLEDGEMENTS

LET'S NOT begin at the beginning. Instead, let's start on February 1, 1995, when Richey James Edwards left his room at the London Embassy Hotel, Bayswater, at 7am. The following day, Edwards was officially reported missing, and on February 17 his car was found abandoned at a service station near the Severn bridge. There are few certainties and plenty of rootless theories. Richey Manic walked out of his hotel, a commitment to a tour, a band and the lives of his family and friends. He walked out of his own world. He has not been heard from since.

The Manic Street Preachers have rarely been out of the glaring eye of the media since they grabbed the beast by the throat and showed it how to do its job.

"From Day One, the Manics wrote their own reviews, dictated their own agenda" (Simon Price, Melody Maker).

More than any other band of their era, their supreme skills of articulation have relegated journalists to the role of mere scribes. If anyone can tell their story, they can. "There's no part of my body that has not been used," they sang of their own prostitution in 'Yes' (from 1994's 'The Holy Bible'). They have bared their soul for the public, unconditionally.

Manic Street Preachers: Design For Living is a straightforward biography. A potted history with understanding and, as promised to their management company, integrity. Nothing more or less will do for a group of people who have revealed, often at their own cost, so much of themselves. Where the facts are uncomfortable or painful, I chose to use the band's own words. Why use anyone else's speculation?

"Those who speak do not know, and those who know do not speak" (Carlos Castaneda, quoted by Richey, talking about Sean).

The voice 'hidden from history' is Sean's. Having been quite happy to let the others take over in interviews, it is only now that there are only three of them that he has felt it appropriate to talk. The balance of the book's contents are therefore in line with how much of themselves the band have allowed to be exposed at any given time.

Their story has been split by events and phases which appear to be distinctive, and I have dissected them accordingly and appropriately. Where there are external reference points, I have tried to explain them as simply and succinctly as possible to bring out the depth of the band's rich intellect.

Leaving aside the ongoing tensions and expectations the band inevitably bring with them, here is an opportunity to see the whole picture. This is neither the story of Richey Edwards nor a history of the band without him. Design For Living promises nothing more than a chronology and nothing less than a narrated biography. It aims to see what Melody Maker's Stud Brothers described as "a whirlwind of contradictions" – those inconsistencies which only serve to make the Manic Street Preachers all the more endearing.

"But then there's the dichotomy; was that what made us such a fantastic band?" (Nicky Wire, Melody Maker).

The Manic Street Preachers are, as Jennifer Nine so aptly described, a "Magic Eye band" in which we can see whatever we choose to. Happy viewing...

Paula Shutkever
June 1996

CHAPTER ONE

BLACKWOOD AND BEYOND

"1 F YOU built a museum to represent Blackwood, all you could put in it would be shit. We used to meet by this opening called Pen-Y-Fan. It was built when the mines closed but now the water has turned green and slimy. They put 2,000 fish in it, but they died. There's a whirlpool in the middle where about two people drown every year" (Nicky, VOX).

"Who wants a world in which the guarantee that we shall not die of starvation entails the risk of dying of boredom?" (Raoul Vaneigem).

"Where we come from, there's a natural melancholy in the air. Everybody, ever since you could comprehend it, felt pretty much defeated. You've got the ruins of heavy industry all around you, you see your parents' generation all out of work, nothing to do, being forced into the indignity of going on courses of no relevance. Like a 50-year-old miner, worked in a pit all his life, there's not much joy for him to go and learn how to type. It's just pointless. And that is all around us, ever since we were born" (Richey, Melody Maker).

Well, they'd never have got a job in their local Tourist Office. It's 1986, and the small mining community of Blackwood, with a population of around a thousand, is under attack by the police. There is a miner's strike on. Four working-class boys are sitting in a bedroom playing music, talking about literature, the political turmoil that's going on outside the window and Apocalypse Now. The sound of 'Baggy' has infiltrated the ears of the record-buying public, and the only well-known musicians to have come out of Wales have been Tom Jones and Shakin' Stevens.

It's grim out west.

"We were worse than alone because the only other band had been The Alarm, so we were like minus ten at the start..." (Nicky, Dazed And Confused).

But the young men in the bedroom aren't listening to the Happy Mondays. There's also an

"Who wants a world in which the guarantee that we shall not die of starvation

anniversary; it's been ten years since punk exploded, and Tony Wilson is hosting a documentary of clips culled from So It Goes, the late-'70s Granada TV show which championed the Sex Pistols and The Clash.

James Dean Bradfield (born 21/2/69), his cousin Sean Moore (30/7/70), and their school friends Nicholas Jones (20/1/69) and Richard James Edwards (22/12/66) are the teenagers in question. They are

sitting in James and Sean's bedroom in Blackwood. Within a few years all the local mines in their area will have been closed and it will be a faceless new town with Aiwa, Toshiba and Sony factories rehiring the ex-miners on short-term contracts to avoid paying out any redundancies. Gwent has the highest alcohol-poisoning rate in the country. The future looks bleak.

"I don't think we could have done this if we hadn't grown up in a shit-hole, where the only way to escape was to create your own reality" (Nicky, Volume).

Having met at Pontypridd Junior School, all four went on to Oakdale Comprehensive, then Crosskeys Tertiary College. Theirs were fairly ordinary childhoods. Nicky and Richey grew up on opposite sides of the same street, where they played football against one another every week for a trophy Nicky's dad found on a rubbish tip. "Because he was so cuddly," Nicky named his football opponent "Teddy" Edwards.

Nicky captained the under-16 Welsh soccer team and had trials for Arsenal and the Welsh Youth Team. Sean left his parents, after they had split up, when he was 13 and went to live with

"We just generally had a blissful childhood, really..."

his cousin, James. Sean became the youngest cornet player in the South Wales jazz orchestra, which played in Newbridge, while James was into drama and sang in the school choir. They are remembered by their contemporaries as being bookworms. Pretty typical stuff, really.

"We just generally had a blissful childhood, really... Especially Richey – up until he was about 16, when he just hit the wall. I don't know, maybe that's what fucked us up. Not that we had bad childhoods, but that our childhoods were too good – we weren't just reading books or watching films, experiencing second-hand culture, we were, y'know, building a dam, messing around in dirt – things like that, which, looking back, seemed much more worthwhile" (Nicky, Melody Maker).

Richey, a shy and withdrawn adolescent, moved in with his grandmother for a short while before moving back to his parents' bungalow at the foot of a steep cul-de-sac in Blackwood. Richey's first problems may have arisen after he was forced to got to church as a teenager – at least, according to Nicky, who thought his football buddy hated it.

"A lot of people had terrible childhoods, but personally, up to the age of 13, I was ecstatically happy. People treated me very well, my dog was beautiful, I lived with my nana and she was beautiful... Then I moved from my nan's and started a comprehensive school and everything started going wrong" (Richey, NME).

When Richey was 14, the IRA began staging protests at a prison in Belfast. Richey was reportedly fascinated by one prisoner in particular – Bobby Sands. Belfast-born, Sands joined the IRA in 1972. After a five-year imprisonment for possession of guns he was given a 14-year jail sentence after the bombing of a furniture factory. While in jail at Long Kesh, better known as the Maze prison, he went on hunger-strike as a demonstration after the authorities refused to acknowledge either himself or other IRA inmates as "political" prisoners. After 66 days, Sands became the first of ten hunger-strikers to die during the summer of 1981.

1tails the risk of dying of boredom?"

"(Sands) made a better statement than anything else that was going on at the time, because it was against himself" (Richey, Melody Maker).

Bobby Sands was one of the first iconic figures that the group drew reference from. As the history of the Manic Street Preachers developed, so, too, would their reclamation of cultural figures continue. The people they mention in both their songs and in interviews say much about their politics, inspirations and place in time.

Several years later, when 12 pits in the valley closed during the miners' strikes, Nicky began writing poetry. He put it together and played it as a song with James when he was 15. "Terrible" is the word he now uses to describe his first set of political lyrics.

Together, Nicky and James would devour culture, reading avidly the likes of William Burroughs, Hunter S Thompson and Jack Kerouac. For music, they'd go to a club in Port Talbot to hear bands of the period, such as Echo And The Bunnymen and The Smiths. They pored over the music press: "Music was the most important thing in our lives," Richey later confessed.

However, in years to come, each member of the band would reminisce about the depressive state of Blackwood and the difference

they felt it made to the paths they took. "This ain't rock'n'roll – this is a hillside," one NME journalist said of Blackwood. There was no romanticism of gritty urban realism when, at the end of 1994, Richey looked back at his roots...

"Blackwood is scarred – industrially, economically and politically. Everything about Blackwood stands as a reminder of 15 years of decay. That affects your world-view for the rest of your life, wherever you go. All the big buildings in Blackwood used to be Miner's Institutes. Now they've been turned into leisure centres and cinemas – and no amount of posters for The Mask can alter the fact. The whole landscape, too; they try and put grass over all the slag heaps, and every time it rains, they turn into huge muddy slides – the landscape is swallowed by a huge slap of blackness" (Time Out).

James later claimed that the band's class was their underlying inspiration and the thing that differentiated them from other bands. Blackwood's community put a big emphasis on education, with the collieries donating money to provide swimming pools and libraries. In Newport there still stands one of the original miners' libraries, set up in 1904. The engraving over the door reads, "LIBRARIES GAVE US POWER" – a slogan the band always remembered and which eventually provided the stimulus for their 1996 single, 'A Design For Life'.

Education was important to the band, too. James got three A levels, and began work at a local bar. Sean, with his A level in music, worked in the civil service. Nicky got As and Bs in his, and escaped to Portsmouth Polytechnic. He found he'd already read all the books on the curriculum and transferred to Swansea University three weeks later to study politics. In the year above him was Richey, with ten GCSEs and three A-grade A levels to his credit, studying political history. Nicky remembers this as a "not very rock'n'roll" period, when they spent time playing golf and Richey "once dressed up as semen for Rag Week, and painted himself all white." (Nicky, NME Student Guide). Shaven-headed, James and Nicky spent a while busking in Cardiff, and all four kept in touch regularly by post.

In 1988 James, Sean and Nicky, joined by a rhythm guitarist called Flicker, began playing together in a band they named Betty Blue. James, for one, had always thought it was inevitable that he would form a band. "I wanted to be someone like Napoleon," he told Volume. "Then I discovered music – or The Clash, to be more precise – and that was it. My destiny was determined."

At that point, Richey was just the band's driver. The band pooled their dole checks together and went to SBS Studio, paying a special "mates-rates", to record their first single, 'Suicide Alley'. 'Tennessee' and 'Repeat After Me', not included on the single, were also recorded. The band pressed 300 copies themselves, giving Richey the task of designing the sleeve, half of which were hand made. The press release, written by Richey, was typically incendiary: "We are the suicide of the non-generation." By August 1990 Steven Wells had made it Single Of The Week in the NME. It was to be their first of many.

Newbridge Hotel was the scene of their first less-than-salubrious gig, supporting a goth band, and a slot at Blackwood's Little Theatre followed. It ended with the Manics being booed off under a hail of cans while the audience chanted, "Simple Minds! Simple Minds!" It was hardly the stuff of dreams. In December 1989, while The Farm and The Happy Mondays were riding high in the charts, it was decided that Flicker's services were no longer required. Richey immediately joined the band – legend has it because he was good-looking and had a great guitar. The quality of his playing was immaterial; his instrument would always be mixed down on stage.

In the meantime, Nicky moved over to bass and Richey changed their name to the Manic

Street Preachers. Their designs to put the glam back into Glamorgan began.

It was during his time as a student that Richey first began to show signs of his self-abusive tendencies. Insomnia had already set in by the end of his first term, and when he told his friends he was having problems sleeping, they suggested having a drink to help. "I drank functionally," Richey told Time Out later. He was also becoming a loner and preferred not to spend much time with other students – to him, living in the university's halls of residence was "a really bad experience" (VOX). It was around this time that James remembers his friend harming himself for the first time – while revising for an exam, Richey cut himself across the chest with a compass.

By 1988, Richey was verging on anorexic.

He was 22 years old and weighed just under six stone.

GENERATION TERRORISTS

AGE OF DARKNESS
REVIEWING THE SITUATIONISM

H AVING GRADUATED with a 2:1 degree ("So it wasn't 100 per cent success, but I got through it," Richey told VOX), he and the rest of the band began their attack on the music world. In 1989, thanks to Richey's persistence in hassling promoter Kevin Pierce, the Manics played their first London date at The Horse And Groom in Great Portland Street. Pierce's curiosity had been aroused by their press release, so he offered them a slot supporting The Claim. As fate would have it, St Etienne's Bob Stanley, then a Melody Maker journalist, saw the gig, liked the band's grim but glamorous image, their hand-painted, sloganised T-shirts (reminiscent of Malcolm McLaren and Vivienne Westwood's DIY punk clothing) and interviewed them for the paper.

The piece began the band's showdown with music past.

"We're not the fucking Senseless Things. We don't want to return to some supposed golden day like they do. You hear bands like that and they talk as if now is useless and everything in 1977 was so great. We're now. All you can do with the past is to never want to be like it. 'Cos the past has created what we're living in now, and we're not happy, so it must've failed" (Richey, Melody Maker).

Nicky was so chuffed with the piece, he sent Stanley a thank you letter – the first the journalist had ever received. Several months later, in December 1989, the band's money stretched as far as 40 minutes' worth of studio time and the Manics recorded a demo. 500 copies of 'New Art Riot' and 'Repeat After Me' (later released as 'Feminine Is Beautiful' and put out by Stanley on his Caff label) were subsequently pressed.

Also impressed by the Horse And Groom gig was Ian Ballard, manager of the Damaged Goods label, who wrote to James asking for a copy of 'Suicide Alley'. After hearing it, he offered them a deal over a handshake, rather than a contract, in January 1990. Ballard later said that one of the things he had most admired about the band, and Richey in particular, was their intellect.

"I think [Richey] finds it difficult talking to people who aren't similarly educated. He'd sit there quoting things and I'd be nodding, thinking, 'I don't know what you're talking about...'" (Select).

With their cut and paste slogans and discursive style, the Manic Street Preachers, by their name alone, have always recognised their political debts, confused as they may be. Part of their motivation came from the Situationist Internationale; a group of Paris-based radical intellectuals who rejected older left-wing views. Formed in 1957 from the ashes of the Lettrist group of 1952, the SI were inspired by Surrealism and Dadaism. They wanted to break down barriers between art and everyday life, between actors and spectators, between producers and consumers. They wanted people to live not as an object but as a subject of history. The Situationists were looking for a revolution of the imagination.

In 1967, Guy Debord, one of the major parties involved with the SI, wrote a groundbreaking book, titled The Society Of The Spectacle, in which he argued for the use of revolutionary slogans and subversion through graphics. Debord argued that capitalism had reduced life to a spectacle – just as Karl Marx had shown how capitalism had alienated the work force from their product. The SI argued for the reinvention of everyday life by the construction of a disruptive situation which would jolt people out of their boredom; they wanted to be the catalyst for a revolution and then disappear. Following much the same spirit, the Manics later announced that they were going to make one album, become world-famous and then split up. Taking his logic to extremes, Guy Debord shot himself through the heart in 1994, and within three days, two of his closest friends were also found dead. Rumours of a suicide pact still circulate.

The Situationists' ideals were a major influence on students during the Paris riots of 1968. Their slogans and cartoons were pasted onto the walls of the city in precisely the way Debord foresaw: a radical subversion of language both textually and graphically. Four years later, in 1972, the SI disbanded, but their influence has seeped through to the '90s. Feminists, anarchists and punks alike have all paid their dues to the French intellectuals. Manchester's Haçienda club derives it name from the writings of Situationist Ivan Chetcheglov who, after being excluded from the Lettrist International, demanded a new theoretical base in The Formula For A New Urbanism, stating metaphorically, "The haçienda must be built." When Tony Wilson opened the club in May 1982 he had the interior decorated in the same colours as a city street.

Wilson's Factory Records also sponsored an exhibition of Situationism at the ICA in 1988. One of the label's bands, The Durutti Column, took their name from a comic-strip created by Andre Bertrand, which recounted the story of the student takeover using Situationist ideals. The Sex Pistols, their designer Jamie Reid, Malcolm McLaren and The Clash were all well-versed in the notions of the SI – and so were the Manics, who went one step further, updating the DIY ethics of punk, writing their own letters to the press and spraying slogans over their bodies.

"We're not left-wing but we do have roots in Situationism and stuff, and when we formed the band, the miners' strike was going on on our doorsteps. So I think when you listen to

'Archives of Pain' [from 'The Holy Bible'], a very right-wing song.... it shows how fucked-up and confused our times are. And it shows that we're still arrogant and unafraid enough to make judgements, even miscalculated ones" (James, Q).

Lyricised by Richey and articulated in James' passionate vocal, it is sometimes arguable whether the band's complex political beliefs can be heard above their sound. Or is that part of the point?

Writing about punk, Dave Laing has asserted that "by excluding the musicality of singing, the possible contamination of the lyric message by the aesthetic pleasure offered by melody, harmony, pitch and so on, is avoided" (Laing, 1985).

That's not to say that James hasn't always made his singing tuneful – it's just often very loud, too. So it's probably a good thing that the Manics have always included lyric sheets with their albums so that the message is always available.

The Manics clearly thought they had the ideological arena to themselves. Richey told VOX that he thought that, politically, there wasn't so much economic poverty as a "poverty of ideas", which meant that no one was satisfied. "We are just another band in the racks but with more intelligence," he added. Being so aware of their own roots also meant they were very sure of who they could and couldn't speak for.

"We can only really make basic, straightforward white rock music, 'cos we're not patronising people. We don't pretend we understand the street, or pretend to understand New York City. You know, we live in a crap little town in Britain" (Richey, Rage).

That's not to say they weren't inspired by bands outside their immediate milieu. Nicky often said that Public Enemy were the band that got him interested in African-American rights, that it made him feel "militant" again. The Manics, perhaps more than any other group of this decade, were also very articulate about their influences outside of the music field. They devoured the Beat writers, sometimes using Allen Ginsberg's poem 'Howl' at gigs, and read voraciously. By the time of their first major feature in the NME they were citing writers like French Existentialist Albert Camus and the American gonzo journalist Hunter S Thompson as influences, as well as making disparaging comments about the state of music in general, and The House of Love in particular.

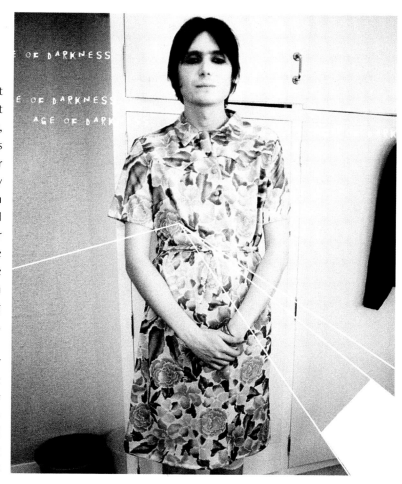

Visually, they held themselves up for dissection. As well as having the rhetoric of The Clash and the militancy of Public Enemy, Nicky and Richey were also incredibly camp – homoerotic even – wearing women's clothes and an abundance of make-up. So much so that Nicky, who at this point was still playing a £10 guitar, was likened to a panda.

"If you're hopelessly depressed like I was, dressing up is just the ultimate escape... nothing could excite me except attention so I'd dress up as much as I could. Outrage and boredom just go hand in hand" (Nicky, Gay Times).

"The Manic Street Preachers are a kamikaze dive-bomber flown by Andy Pandy and his transsexual friend" (Steven Wells, NME).

They hadn't been the only musicians to cross-dress. From Mick Jagger on the cover of 'Have You Seen Your Mother Baby Standing In The Shadow' and Bowie's 'The Man Who Sold The World' there have been a whole host of other benders of gender: Boy George, Marilyn, Annie Lennox, Michael Stipe, Nirvana, Andy Bell and kd lang. And certainly Suede's androgynous approach had already been highly successful. Jon Savage, cultural rock critic and author as well as great fan of the band, felt the band had seen "the transformational possibilities inherent in pop" (The Times).

They were the opposite of the laddishness and hooliganism that some of the Madchester brigade had brought out. In a piece for Gay Times, Richard Smith explained their cross-over, "frock'n'roll" appeal by saying that "the Preachers fly in the face of fashion by playing 'manly' rock music whilst coming on like absolute jessies."

Their own press releases used quotes from the likes of Greil Marcus, William Burroughs and even Karl Marx. While they clearly had a sedate academic side, their live performance was frenetic to the point of being deranged. Nicky scissor-kicked around the stage, making mouthy interjections, whilst James virtually shattered his larynx, Richey gave Keith Richards a run for his money and Sean, solidly and subdued, just got on with the job of beating the living daylights out of his drum kit. The mayhem produced on stage, by osmosis, encouraged their audience to do likewise and sent reviewers into overdrive.

"The Manics flap and scream and jump and have brutal, loving sexual intercourse with their instruments as if it is three seconds to midnight on the Chemical Warfare Clock and entrance to heaven is only guaranteed to cute little boys with ruptured vocal chords and sore cocks" (Steven Wells, NME).

With their relatively bare stage sets – just a back row of Marshall stacks and a raised drum kit – the band took on the same simple punk persona of over a decade before. This particular piece of Wells' prose was part of a review of The Throbs at London's Marquee, where the Manics were supporting. The journalist spent so much time raving about them, he only left 35 words to sum up the main band. He later noted the band's many contradictions. Most pointedly, they implored others to denounce the age of consumption when they were such shameless culture-vultures themselves. On the one hand, he thought, behaving like anti-heroes, when their music could be said to be populist, worked in their favour.

"They are inconsistent, contradictory, totally fucked-up and 100 per cent sincere. If that doesn't excite you then I don't know why you are still interested in pop music" (Steven Wells, NME).

"We are the only band that reserve the right to contradict ourselves" (Manic Street Preachers fanzine).

The pattern of contradictions begins to take form.

"I've never hurt anyone. I might smash a guitar on stage, but I only ever damage myself... I've never raised my voice to anybody, but most of my interviews read like a Scorsese script" (Richey, Time Out).

But then, many saw this in a positive light, as a refusal to be pigeon-holed.

"The Manics' triumph is that where they could have been the full stop at the end of rock'n'roll, they chose to be its question mark" (Taylor Parkes, Melody Maker).

Melody Maker's Stud Brothers take the credit for being the first journalists to cover the group, and remember receiving, in 1989, a tape, a letter and a promise of drugs if they went to visit them in Blackwood.

"The tape was so rough-cut and ready, it was almost unlistenable, a grim but brutally energetic rendition of what would be their first single, 'Motown Junk'" (Stud Brothers, Melody Maker).

In April 1990 the band recorded 'UK Channel Boardroom' as a free flexi-disc with a fanzine called Goldmining. The B-side was a song called 'Vision Of Dead Desire', which they later revamped as 'You Love Us'. In an interview with Melody Maker the same month, Richey began a pattern of asserting how much better his group were, compared to any other band:

"We wanna be the biggest rock'n'roll nightmare ever. We'll do whatever is required..

"Everyone likes Happy Mondays 'cos when the working class dance, it means nothing except prole fashion. The Stone Roses seem to understand the working class, but only in interviews. No one is speaking for people like us" (Melody Maker).

Two months late, Ian Ballard, true to his handshake, put out the 'New Art Riot' EP with 'Strip It Down', 'Teenage 20/20' and 'Last Exit Yesterday'. Originally only 1,000 copies were released because the band, perfectionists as ever, were not totally happy with it. It wasn't until six months later that it was re-released on CD, when it received its first review in the NME, which described them as "a bunch that have only ever been described as 'Welsh gits' but in fact make Birdland look like a bunch of cissies." A copy of the EP was also sent to Philip Hall, founder of the London-based management and independent press company Hall Or Nothing, who at that time was managing the likes of The Stone Roses. The EP impressed him enough to make him drive up to see them rehearse at a local comprehensive school in South Wales. Philip and his brother, Martin Hall (who ran the management side of the company) were to become much more than business associates; more like an extended family.

"We really had no notion of what Philip did, or how helpful he could be to us. We just thought he sounded like a person who could help us out. Within three months he'd become our manager, we escaped from Wales and the four of us slept on his floor in London for six months. He had to put up with a lot... and at least before he died we'd repaid the faith he'd put into us by starting to become a successful band" (Nicky, Volume).

Without being asked, Hall lent the band over £40,000 after remortgaging his home – a home that the band moved, en masse, into in January of 1992, only a few months after Hall had married his partner, Terri. In return, they would clean the house and prepare tea for their hosts – the perfect guests. Alarmingly, Richey would also cut himself in front of the others while watching television, stopping and apologising if anyone objected. He was, as one journalist later put it "subconsciously [drawing] blood in the same way others would chew their nails" (Select).

All through June and August of the same year the band played support slots with The Family Cat and The Cranes. The 'Welsh Clash' tag had already begun to stick, and in interviews the group were getting tired of having to explain themselves. They were adamant that they were very much a group of the moment, that they were a "different generation" (VOX). It took two years before the Manics finally shook off the Clash comparisons.

"This may not be the new voice of London Calling, but taken as the bark and snap of young rock pups, it ain't 'arf bad" (Lenny Stoute, Toronto Star).

As early as August 1990, when 'Stay Beautiful' was released, Steven Wells declared in the NME that "they will be the most important rock band in the world", on the grounds that "they have more anger and energy than any other band I have ever interviewed" (NME). Powerful stuff indeed. The band's first feature in the NME was indicative of the period, spewing out venom at everyone, everything including themselves:

"We wanna be the biggest rock'n'roll nightmare ever. We'll do whatever is required and give you the biggest ever posthumous record sales... We are the scum that remind people of misery. When we jump on stage it is not rock'n'roll cliché but the geometry of contempt... We are the decaying flowers in the playgrounds of the rich. We are young, beautiful scum, pissed off with the world." (NME).

The letters they sent to the press argued that they had the same "scum factor" as the Happy Mondays.

"People we met in London would never like the idea of meeting a girl in the pub and having a bag of chips and a fuck in the bus stop on the way home. That's something ordinary working-class people do all the time. We'd do that; we wouldn't check into a hotel – it'd be, 'Stop here a minute, I want my dick sucked.' That's the scum factor" (NME).

Throughout their career, the Manics have always been a double-edged sword, a mass of contradictions, and they were easily in danger of becoming a of rock'n'roll cliché. People loved them or hated them for it.

"It's perfect. Just how it should be. I'm just as happy having people loathe me as I am to have them love me. Music's got so safe and ordinary, it'd be good if a few more bands tried to get those sort of opinions forced on them" (Richey, Gay Times).

There was no other option. Fortunately, Jeff Barrett of Heavenly Records positioned himself firmly on the 'love them' side of the fence. Having heard of them through Hungry Beat fanzine, he read one of their very inspiring letters – which moved him more than their music did, evidently – and he eventually went to see them play at London's Rock Garden. At this time, the band were still undertaking 'pay-to-play' gigs, so when Barrett offered them a deal in August, again with a handshake, they accepted within a month. Their live shows, even then, were what sold the band. Andy Peart said of their gig at the Bull & Gate in London that he hadn't seen such an "exhilarating" band since Birdland: "The difference is, I'm convinced the Manic Street Preachers mean it." Many journalists were stunned, including Melody Maker's Dave Simpson:

"But, in a sense, I'm for all this. Really. I like it that a bunch of kids can get up on stage and irritate people like they're irritating me. There's something very healthy about a new generation telling the previous one to get stuffed."

In October 1990 they recorded one of their live favourites, 'Motown Junk', as a single, with 'Sorrow 16' and 'We, Her Majesty's Prisoners' set for the B-side. The single earned its notoriety with its line about laughing when John Lennon was shot, and so began Nicky Wire's tirades against other musicians who he felt bore no relevance to his life. 'Motown Junk' later made NME's prestigious Single of the Week slot the following January, and before the year was out, the band had their Town & Country Club 2 show recorded for BBC2's Snub TV, when they told the nation they wanted to mix politics and sex, look good and say brilliant things. "We'll never write a love song, ever. We'll be dead before we have to do that," they promised.

"We don't even want to reach the music papers, we just want to reach The Sun, The Star, The

"I cut myself to show that we are no gimmick."

Mirror. That's what most people read. We'd rather be sensationalised than just be another NME band and get critical respect. Critical respect is the easiest thing to get in the world because journalists are so crap."

As the Manics set up their first headline tour, Nicky Wire wasn't too happy. The first four dates of the February tour were cancelled as he had a thyroid cyst removed from his neck, and returning to the tour too quickly brought on a relapse. By the end of March 1991 the band had played the Paris Locomotive club, as part of a Heavenly package tour, with Flowered Up, East Village and St Etienne. It was here that they first trashed their equipment.

Their third NME Single of the Week came with 'You Love Us', immediately hailed as another classic. "Let's not mince words here," wrote the reviewer, "this is a motherfucker of a single... It sends shivers down my spine just thinking about the Manic Street Preachers. Secretly, I'm sure everyone wants to be in this band, living out all their sordid rock'n'roll fantasies. They just won't admit it" (NME).

On May 15, 1991, the Manics played Norwich Arts Centre. The gig would go down in rock history. Radio 1 DJ Steve Lamacq was writing for NME at the time and went down to cover the gig. After speaking to the band for around half an hour, Steve told them he thought some people might regard them "as just not for real" (NME). Richey, wearing a T-shirt sprayed with the words 'Spectators Of Suicide', pulled out a razor-blade and slowly, and with deliberation, carved '4 REAL' into his left forearm, saying, "We're not the next Birdland, we do mean what we do".

"We carried on talking for another three or four minutes," said Lamacq, "and by that time he

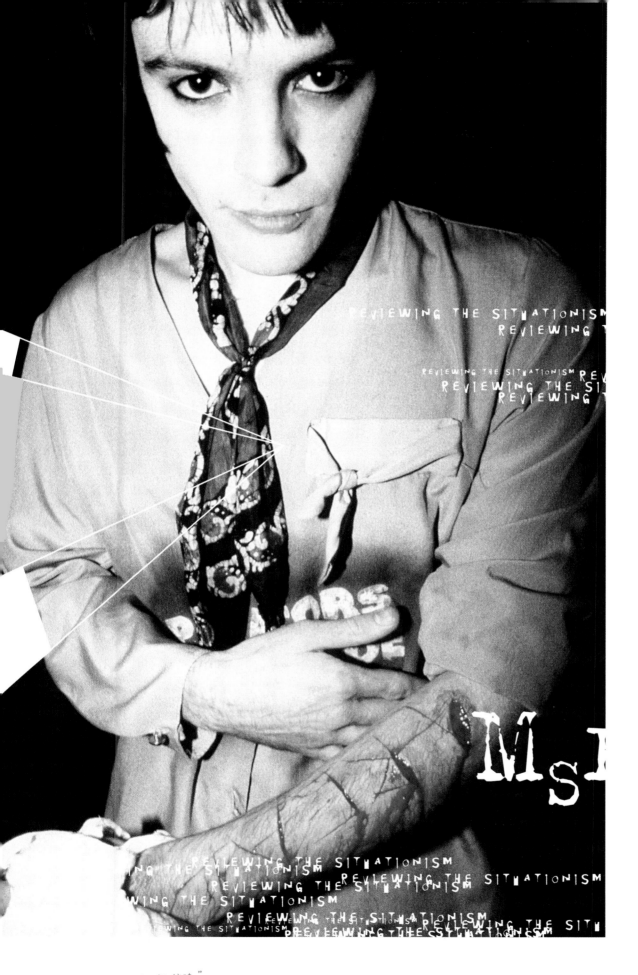

REVIEWING THE SITUATIONISM

REVIEWING T

REVIEWING THE SITUATIONISM REV

REVIEWING THE SI

REVIEWING T

M s

REVIEWING THE SITUATIONISM
ING THE SITUATIONISM
REVIEWING THE SITUATIONISM
REVIEWING THE SITUATIONISM
WING THE SITUATIONISM
REVIEWING THE SITUATIONISM REVIEWING THE SITU
EWING THE SITUATIONISM REVIEWING THE SITU
REVIEWING THE SITUATIONISM

ll be dead before we have to do that."

was dripping blood all over the carpet" (VOX). A few years later, Lamacq said that what was so eerie about it all was that Richey was so placid.

"He didn't look in any pain whatsoever. One of the things that was so strange and frightening about it was that he was so calm. You didn't even feel like he was making a point. He could have almost been writing it in Biro" (Select).

In shock, Lamacq eventually gathered his wits about him, got their manager and helped organise an ambulance to take Richey to Norwich General Hospital, where he was given 17 stitches. Richey insisted that other patients were treated before him. The following day, having had to cancel that night's gig in Birmingham, Richey rang and apologised to the journalist for

"He didn't look in any pain whatsoever. One of the things that was so strange an

any distress he might have caused.

"You have to put it into the context of where we come from. Back there, people don't believe in bands anyway... the thing for us is, it's really hard to convince you that we are for real. I know you don't like us, but we are for real. When I was a teenager I never had a band who said anything about my life, that's why we're doing this. Where we came from, we had nothing" (Richey, NME).

"I cut myself to show that we are no gimmick. When I couldn't convince a certain person that we were not a joke band, I did that to myself to show him. Maybe people will now realise what we are all about, but I don't regret it and, no, I don't feel a prat" (Richey, Daily Star).

When Lamacq arrived at the NME office, and Ed Sirrs, the photographer who took shots that night, brought his roll of colour transparencies in, a debate over decency ensued. Journalist Andrew Collins thought Richey was an "idiot", whereas James Brown, now editor of Loaded, was more enthusiastic, saying, "We've got to print that. It's rock'n'roll... I think more bands should do that sort of thing. It's artistic expression."

The photographs were used, in full colour. In the printed piece, Lamacq said he thought it was a "dumb way to end an evening", that it was as stupid as the spontaneity of Sid Vicious, and signed off the review by saying, "DON'T BE DAFT BASTARDS."

It was an incident Richey would often be called upon to defend.

"I tried talking to Steve for an hour to explain ourselves. He saw us as four hero-worshipping kids trying to replicate our favourite bands. There was no way I could change his mind. I didn't abuse him or insult him. I just cut myself. To show that we are no gimmick, that we are pissed off, that we are for real" (Richey, NME).

Just under a year later, Richey told The Guardian that his self-harm was indicative of his class:

"People should realise what the level of violence is like in most people's lives. It's said that working class resentment is always turned on itself; nobody seems to realise that."

Here, again, the paradoxical side of the Manics comes through. On the one hand they strove to be hugely successful; on the other, at least one member was hell-bent on self-destruction. The event never really died down; years later, Richey was still being asked about it.

"I didn't know what I could possibly say to him to make him understand... Other bands hit journalists, and it's very macho... I would never do that" (Richey, Q).

"I never shout at anybody. So if I cut myself or stub a cigarette out on my arm, to me, it's a release. If somebody pushes me or punches me when I'm out in Cardiff, that hurts me more than having a couple of stitches in my arm. I'm weak. All my life I've felt weak compared to other people. If they want to crush me, they can. But I know I can do things that other people

frightening about it was he was so calm. He could almost have been writing it in Biro."

can't." (Richey, Select).

Four days later, on May 21, 1991, the band signed their contract to Sony for £250,000 plus £400,000 to finance the album. Apologising to Jeff Barrett, the band explained that they didn't want to remain at a fanzine level, they wanted to make it big and at any price. "Signing to a major record company is the price of an education," Nicky said. "We don't care what they do to us. The credibility of indie-labels is shit" (NME).

"We've never been the Trade Unionists of Rock, we know that we could never reach as many people as we wanted, unless it was on a major. We were willing prostitutes" (James, Raw).

As with most bands who move from an independent label to a major, the Manics were under the microscope again, being asked to explain their reasons and accused of selling out. A year later, as they had explained in the lyrics of 'Democracy Coma', they knew that they were owned by Sony and that they could be manipulated by them at will.

"We know they completely own us, they can do anything they want with us, they can drop us... In fact, they said, 'If you want, come in and smash the place up, it would be good press.' It wouldn't be good press. We'd end up paying for it..." (Richey, NME).

Tim Bowen, managing director of Columbia, had seen them at a student-only

gig at Guildford University, and been as inspired as when he'd seen The Clash, who he'd also signed. Explaining why, he said:

"They're more anarchistic than anybody else of their age — or my age, come to that. They have something to say, they're pissed off about where they live, they're pissed off about

REVIEWING THE SITUATIONISM
THE SITUATIONISM
REVIEWING THE SITUATIONISM

REVIEWING THE SITUATIONISM REVIEWING THE SITUATIONISM
REVIEWING THE SITUATIONISM
REVIEWING THE SITUATIONISM
THE SITUATIONISM

REVIEWING THE SITUATIONISM
REVIEWING THE SITUAT
REVIEWING THE SITUATIONISM
REVIEWING THE
REVIEWING THE SITUATIONISM REVIEWING
THE SITUATIONISME THE SITUATION
REVIEWING THE SITUATIONISM

unemployment, but they're not so pissed off that they can't enjoy themselves. And that's what young people are meant to do" (Tim Bowen, NME).

Bowen initiated the Sony contract. The band were to hit the headlines again within weeks. In June, the Manics played Cambridge University's £150-a-head-dinner-jacket affair, Downing College May Ball. All was going well in front of a crowd of 200 students, until, four songs into their set, Richey put his foot on a monitor and staff pulled the PA plug, worried that he was about to trash the equipment. Unwittingly, they were right. Sean began smashing his £1,000 kit and James joined in the fracas, punching a college rugby player. Inevitably, the police were called to disperse the ensuing havoc as the band began a shouting match with the audience, slagging off the Royal Family into the bargain. The tabloids also reported allegations that one of the group had groped two women at the gig. "It was so obscene we walked out in disgust," one student said (Daily Star), whereas another told the NME that the Manics were the best thing all night.

The early years are packed full of tales of gig-mania. At a show at Gourock Bay Hotel, near Glasgow, the Manics were pelted with all kinds of junk – including syringes – by their audience, and as a punter dived onto the drum kit, Sean missed a near-decapitation when the cymbal flew

off its hook. Nicky goaded on the torrents, and pointed out that perhaps their venom and barrage of object-throwing would be better directed at "institutions, not the band".

On April 29, at a support slot with First Offence, at Manchester's Boardwalk, the band told the audience that their first offence was to be beautiful. It was a direct hit at the headlining Manchester band, who had told the press they did not want to be put in the same category as the Blackwood Boys, because "they wear make up, they're faggots. We hate faggots."

On reflection, the band thought that First Offence were threatened by their androgynous appeal: they just couldn't handle it. "We like to threaten people sexually. Especially males," Nicky told Gay Times.

Game, set and well-retorted match to the Manics.

'Stay Beautiful' was released in the July, and became their first Top 40 hit. During the next tour, playing with Daisy Chainsaw at Reading's After Dark Club on August 10, 1991, more classic chaos occurred. One song in, the equipment blew up, the audience heckled ("You wankers!") and James heckled back. Without any stage security on tap, fights broke out between the band, the crew and the audience.

Dressed in their birthday suits for the video of 'Love's Sweet Exile', released in November, Richey continued the band's stand against the rest of the musical world by saying that they would "always hate Slowdive more than Adolf Hitler" (NME). In the same interview it had also been noted that they had no time for Kingmaker, Ned's Atomic Dustbin, Morrissey, Chapterhouse, Moose... you name 'em, the Manics could give you half a dozen reasons why they abhorred them. "We set out to be truly despised and hated," Richey told the press when looking back at how they were just seen to be naming a band and slagging them off (Rage). Around this time, the band appeared on The Word. They had been asked to perform 'Love's Sweet Exile', but they changed their set and played 'Repeat', with its "Fuck Queen and country" line intact. As the Daily Mirror declared, the band threw the programme into confusion, just as the audience threw themselves over one another – including dancers with Bomb The Bass, who had joined in the frenzy. A month later, Nicky was again in hospital, this time with glandular fever, and three more dates were cancelled.

Having been let loose to review the singles in the NME in January 1992, and with the reissue of 'You Love Us', the Manics made their first appearance on Top Of The Pops. "Regard all art critics as useless and dangerous", dictated the quote on the album sleeve next to the track's listing on 'Generation Terrorists'. Taken from the manifesto of the Italian Futurist movement, the sentiments were that modern design was as valid as classic art. Like the Manics' own values, Futurist politics have been problematic; the Futurists were often accused of fascism in that they seemed to celebrate violence and the speed of war.

By this time, the Manics were notching up their national radio sessions, even becoming established through a regular skit on the Steve Wright show.

The following month they released their debut album, 'Generation Terrorists', produced by Steve Brown (who had worked with The Cult) and mixed at The Hit Factory. It was released on February 10. An impressive double-album debut, it was described in the press as "the most ambitious, scene-stealing album of the '90s so far" (NME). An album which Richey reputedly never played a note on, it has since sold over 250,000 worldwide, leading Nicky to describe it as "a perfect statement" (Raw). However, while in the studio recording, Richey kept breaking down into floods of tears. James became increasingly concerned about his friend; when asked what was wrong, Richey explained that he was worried that if the band ever split up, he would be left with nothing. In one of the band's fanzines, Nicky confirmed that James recorded Richey's guitar parts, and added:

"All [Richey] does is go to London, drives around in the Sony limousine, goes to Soho strip joints, spends £300 on the band's AMEX, comes back covered in love-bites and asks how the track's going. I think that's the thing that's given me the most pride in this band."

Every track on 'Generation Terrorists' pointed, with a quote, to the band's immense political and literary awareness. From poets like ee cummings and Philip Larkin, to writers like Orwell and Burroughs, to political groups like the Situationists, there seemed to be a common denominator in their choice: heaviness. Inevitably, they were also great admirers of Sylvia Plath, a 'confessional poet' of great personal intensity who gassed herself at her London home in 1963, after splitting with her poet husband, Ted Hughes. The Manics later used the title of her biography, The Girl Who Wanted To Be God, on their fourth album, 'Everything Must Go'.

With great rhetoric, as is their wont – James once said that "language has always been our weapon" (Volume) – the band said they would make their first album a double, sell more copies than Guns N' Roses' 'Appetite For Destruction', then split up.

"We wanted to sign to the biggest record label in the world, put out a debut album that would sell 20 million and then break up. Get massive and then just throw it all away" (Richey, The Times).

By the next year they'd retracted the statement, and when asked if they'd carry on in spite of their earlier proclamations Richey replied, "Of course we'll do it, because our level of hypocrisy is on the same level of the media and the press."

Hypocrisy is too easy a cop-out. They were quite aware that "in England... the music press

HE SITUATIONISM
REVIEWING THE SITUATIONISM

ING THE SITUATIONISM REVIEWING THE SITUATIONISM
VIEWING THE SITUATIONISM
REVIEWING THE SITUATIONISM

wields the power to make or destroy tastes" (Richey, Toronto Star). A few months earlier, in a weekly diary he'd written for Select, Richey wrote how "breakfast is always sad on a Wednesday," because "the music press arrives." It would be true to say that the Manics, rather than fall victim to the press, had actually worked out how to use it for their own means.

This time, they faced a time of judgement for their album; a trial by ordeal in the music press. They need not have worried. Apart from a review saying it was full of "dreary rock clichés, likely to induce sleep rather than passion" (The Times), most critics were overwhelmed by it. Writing for the NME, Barbara Ellen gave the album an almost unheard of ten-out-of-ten rating. Dismissing allegations of Clash copyism, she said that having no throwbacks to past musicians would be like "expecting human beings to give birth to different shaped babies every time". Greil Marcus had made a similar point in his book, Lipstick Traces:

"The question of ancestry in culture is spurious. Every new manifestation in culture rewrites the past, changes old maudits into new heroes, old heroes into those who should have never been born... but in all times forgotten actors emerge from the past, not as ancestors but as familiars."

Uncertain of how to approach dissecting the social commentary that the lyrics provided Ellen applauded its ambitiousness.

"People who steer too close to the sun often get their wings melted. The great thing is, the Manics dare to fly. So (10) and stuff the marking system." (NME)

Having survived the hyperbole and hype ("They're a stadium band looking for a stadium. And getting close to finding it," noted one NME journalist) and, in spite of their success at the beginning of the year, Richey allowed an insight of his own alienation in his diary piece for Select:

"Early evening I walk around Soho on my own as I have so few friends. It starts to rain. And even cheap dreams don't stop the rain."

He had also told the same magazine a year before that he thought, of the Manics that "...we are the loneliest people I've ever met."

As 'Slash 'N' Burn' went straight into the charts at Number 20 during March, Richey undertook an interview with teen-pop magazine Smash Hits. He told their readers that they should "die before they're too old"; the comment was edited out of the final copy. On March 21, at a gig at Essex University, Richey was so drunk he fell over on stage, Nicky was in pain from an operation on his legs, and James was suffering from a horrific cocktail of flu and hepatitis which made him cough up blood. The show endured power-cuts galore, but the audience didn't care. It had been a riotous tour, and the Manics took a well-deserved break soon after.

The following month the band were invited to the IRMA awards – the Irish equivalent of the Brits – in Dublin, where they played in place of Seal, who had just pulled out. They performed 'You Love Us', James with 'You Hate Us' daubed in red lipstick all over his chest. There's never a dull moment when the Manics are around, and after James had a run-in with one of the TV presenters, the band were unceremoniously thrown out. For Nicky, not once, but twice in one evening – he was later chucked out of the hotel bar for coming in wearing just his boxer shorts. The torrent of publicity the Manics accumulated around this time now seems quite astounding. It was also very well calculated.

"We took a very academic approach at being a band. We were quite clinical. We were like magpies, collecting information, keeping dossiers on journalists and learning how to manipulate them" (James, Volume).

In May, as 'Motorcycle Emptiness', a song about the aftermath of Thatcherism, was released as a single, the band prepared for their first American shows, just after the LA riots. It is reported that some of the Red Hot Chili Peppers were intrigued enough to attend a show. Stuart Bailie, reporting for the NME, heard a very disillusioned Richey moan how he thought "everything", especially sex, "just seems for sale" (NME). Whether he thought he had sold his own soul is up for debate, but Bailie also saw how the effects of self-harm were so visible:

"Early evening I walk around Soho on my own, as I have so few

"You start looking at his right arm; burns, scrapes, slices, lesions – a lurid pink testimony to a sustained programme of self-mutilation" (NME).

A couple of years later, at a gig at Cambridge Corn Exchange, Ryan Gilbey described Richey as "an alcoholic anorexic wearing a scar-tissue suit" (The Independent). But again, Richey diffused the situation, not by covering up the evidence but by speaking so eloquently about it:

"They're just my war wounds. I've always found it hard to express how I feel, even from when I was a little child. It's a very British emotion – they keep things bottled up inside them. Some more than others" (VOX).

On their return to the UK, Sean's personal life was taken apart by the tabloids. Having been estranged from his parents, he had received a letter from them asking for a reconciliation. His response was rage. "Why didn't they want me back then when I needed them? It's too late now and I don't want to be any part of it" (Daily Star).

The Manics next 'situation' occurred during August as they took the stage at the 20th Reading show. In front of 40,000 people, the band came on to Marilyn Monroe's 'I Wanna Be Loved By You' with Nicky, as reserved as ever, wearing a pink Lurex jacket and a black feather boa. This was the first time the band had played 'Suicide Is Painless' live, which went down a storm. Having rubbed his crotch with some vigour during 'You Love Us', Nicky threw his bass into the audience. Unfortunately, it came down heavily on a security man, who ended up needing stitches. The Manics were asked to leave the site straight after their set. They wanted to get home in time for Match Of The Day anyway, they said.

In September 1992 the band released the cover of the theme from the TV series M*A*S*H, 'Suicide Is Painless', which reached the Top Ten and was acclaimed as yet another Single Of The Week in the NME. They had recorded the track for 'Ruby Trax', a charity album celebrating the 40th anniversary of the NME in conjunction with The Spastics Society. The paper said that the song could have been written for them: "'Suicide Is Painless' was an epic just waiting for the Manic Street Preachers to cover it". They chose the song as a reminder of the days when Top Of The Pops went off-air because of the Musicians Union dispute; it was a "very gloomy time in our lives," they said. For a track which they recorded in one day in Cardiff, and cost a mere £80, it did extremely well; it was their first Top Ten hit. It included an extra track, 'Sleeping With The NME', recorded by Radio Five.

At the same time, The Daily Star covered the band's addiction to fruit machines. It was reported that they had lost £100,000 on them (of which Sean's tab was £40,000) and their record company had to bail them out.

"We all love to play the fruit machines but Sean owed thousands of pounds. The problem got so bad our record company had to pay off all our debts for us, and they banned us from gambling ever again" (Richey, Daily Star).

Two months later the band were in the press again with the release of 'Little Baby Nothing', with the backing vocal assistance of American actress Traci Lords, a former porn star. "Traci Lords is female power," Richey proclaimed in Select.

Lords almost brought the American porn industry to a halt when the FBI found out that 39 of her films had been made when she was under 18, the legal age. The band had seen her in Cry

riends. It starts to rain. And even cheap dreams don't stop the rain."

Baby, her most recent film since going mainstream, and Lords, having heard their music and had a brief telephone conversation with Richey, flew in to see them play before recording the track.

"We wanted her or Kylie because at the time they were both women that were perceived as puppets. No one could imagine that they might have their own vision on how they wanted to be sold" (Richey, Select).

On the album, the band added part of Valerie Solanas' manifesto to the track's listing on the LP sleeve. Solanas was a radical feminist of the late '60s who founded the Society for Cutting Up Men (SCUM) and attempted to assassinate Andy Warhol. The quote chosen by the Manics was suitably inflammatory: "The male chromosome is an incomplete female chromosome. In other words, the male is a walking abortion; aborted at the gene stage. To be male is to be deficient, emotionally limited; maleness is a deficiency disease and males are emotional cripples..."

Putting the proverbial cat deep in among the pigeons is one of the Manic Street Preachers' major strengths. It is precisely these highly charged political displays that make the band so attractive to men and women alike (as in "I don't wanna be a man," from 'Life Becoming a Landslide'). Feminists? Misogynists? Who can tell?

Nicky had been pretty quiet for a while, so to round off the end of December 1992, at a gig

"I've got nothing against Michael Stipe at all. I'm just all for bitchin' in music."

at London's Kilburn National Ballroom, he announced that "...In the season of goodwill, let's hope Michael Stipe goes the same way as Freddie Mercury pretty soon." (At this point, rumours were rife that Stipe was HIV-positive.) Unsurprisingly, the comment went down like a lead balloon. "Even by the Manics' mouthy standards, it's a terrible remark" (John Harris, NME).

Backstage, Nicky told everyone that it was a protest of the unquestioned reverence of rock stars and the emptiness of liberal arguments about AIDS, when people like Mick Ronson had terminal cancer. While Richey defended the comment in the press, Sugar frontman Bob Mould spoke out in the NME:

"How big a dickhead does someone have to be to say something that stupid? Are they that desperate for attention? I feel very sorry for them for their naivety, and I feel sorry for their fans for tolerating them... to wish that predicament like that on anyone is very selfish and very useless."

AIDS charity the Terrence Higgins Trust also voiced its concern:

"It's a very nasty thing to wish on anybody. It shows a real lack of health education on his part. It's a very unpleasant thing to say" (Jimmy Glass, THT spokesperson).

In a 'Rock'n'roll Dilemmas' session with Kerrang! magazine, Nicky was asked if he would donate bone marrow to Michael Stipe. "But of course I would," he protested. "I've got nothing against Michael at all. I'm just all for bitchin' in music."

It wasn't until a year later that it became clear that the comment was, in fact, brought on by anguish at seeing their friend and publicity officer Philip Hall battling against cancer.

MSP

THE HOLY BIBLE
MANIC STREET PREACHERS

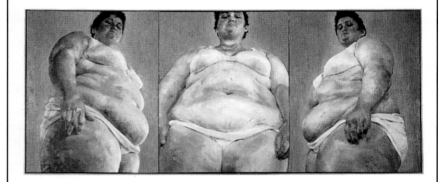

1. YES
2. IFWHITEAMERICATOLDTHETRUTHFORONEDAYIT'SWORLDWOULDFALLAPART
3. OF WALKING ABORTION • 4. SHE IS SUFFERING • 5. ARCHIVES OF PAIN
6. REVOL • 7. 4st 7lb • 8. MAUSOLEUM • 9. FASTER • 10. THIS IS YESTERDAY
11. DIE IN THE SUMMERTIME • 12. THE INTENSE HUMMING OF EVIL • 13. P.C.P.

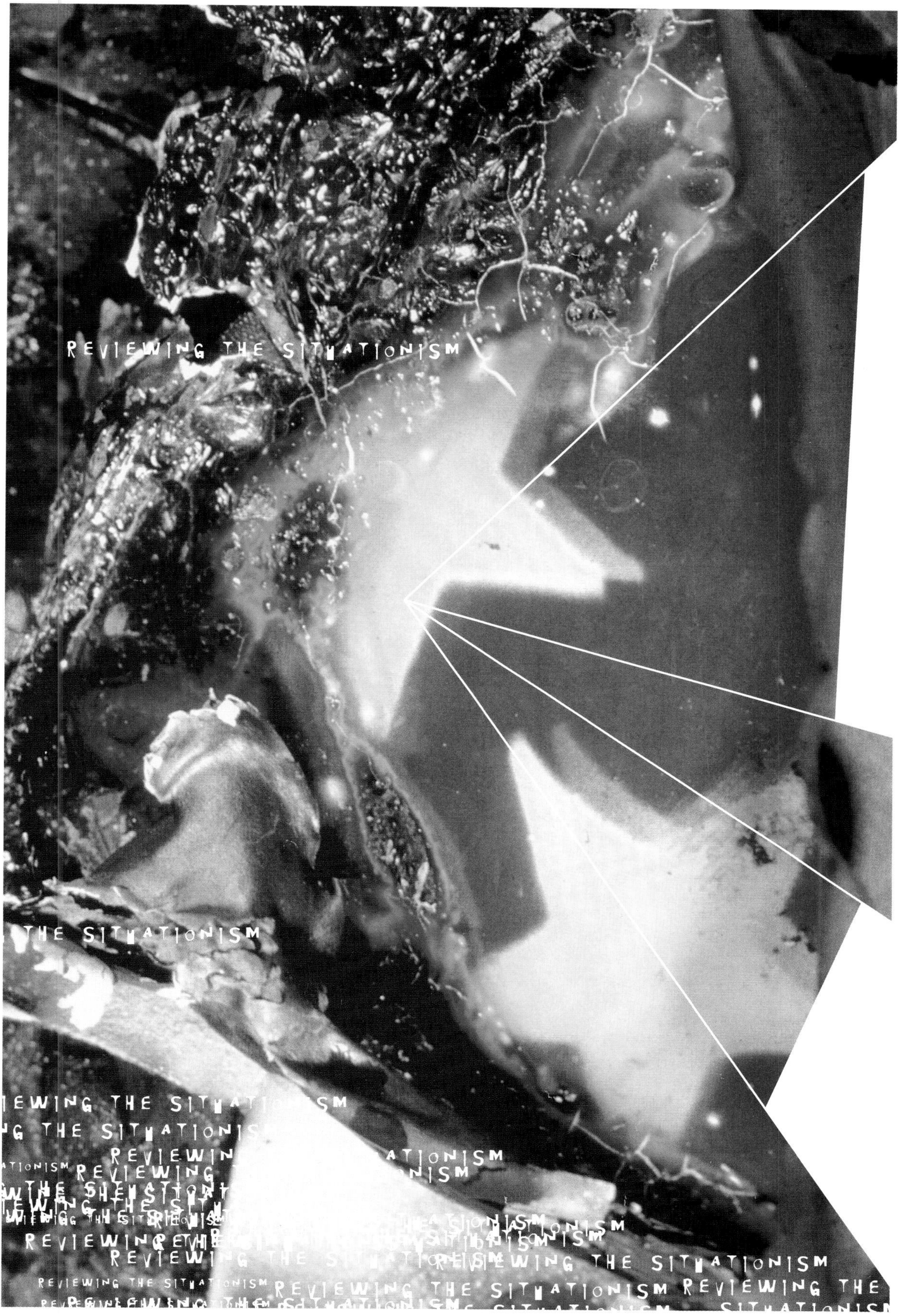
REVIEWING THE SITUATIONISM
THE SITUATIONISM
REVIEWING THE SITUATIONISM
REVIEWING THE SITUATIONISM
REVIEWING THE SITUATIONISM
REVIEWING THE

THE AGE OF (UN) REASON

THE AGE OF (UN) REASON THE AGE OF (UN) REASON
THE AGE OF (UN) REASON THE AGE OF (UN) REASON THE AGE OF (UN) REASO
THE AGE OF (UN) REASONTHE AGE OF (UN) REASON
THE AGE OF (UN) REASON

BY MAKING such wild claims about their debut, the Manics inevitably faced a backlash. "At the time we were giving interviews and saying that to the press, though, we didn't believe it," said Richey. "We knew we couldn't quite do that. But if we had aimed any lower in the beginning, I don't think anyone would've paid as much attention to us" (The Times).

"The whole point was to be hypocritical, to be false" (Richey, Raw).

By the middle of 1993, The Manics had begun a new era. Where once Richey paid more attention to pogoing up and down on stage than he did to playing guitar, he had now made a conscious effort to "master chord progression" (NME). Nicky had become aware that life wasn't a bed of roses; their success didn't mean that everything was going to go away. He had also gone a little "straight-edge"; the rock'n'roll years were behind him. They said goodbye to the make-up and blouses. For at least three of them, their 'Hammer Of The Gods' period was over.

They also made a startling volte-face about the brash comments of the years before ("Every time we talk we come out with Mark E Smith-isms," Richey told the NME):

"Everybody knows that the Mondays made some fucking great records, but we could never say that, because it was our blinkered Pol Pot period, and we didn't like what they were supposed to represent" (Richey, NME).

Rather than a band that were going to change the world, they had become more accepting of of their position in it:

"I've never thought a band could ever do anything that important. It can change individuals, it can create a common ground for important issues, but in terms of actually doing something, changing the economic infrastructure, it's not gonna do that, it never has done" (Richey, NME).

At the same time, Richey's mental health was still an issue. While he had spent time at health farms, he was also known to

"The whole point was to be hypocritical, to be false."

have stubbed cigarettes out on his arm. As far as his drinking was concerned he, once more, told the press that it was to help with insomnia, in the same way people went to the pub to forget about the pressures of work.

"I just want to forget about things when it starts getting dark. It's pretty impossible to sleep unless you've taken something" (Richey, NME).

June 1993 also saw the release of their second album, 'Gold Against The Soul', and their single 'From Despair To Where'. A far cry from pooling their Giros, the band recorded the album in a Surrey studio at the cost of £2,000 a day, replete with snooker tables and swimming pools. Just to add to their incongruities, they also recorded some parts in a Cardiff studio based in the city's red-light district. As with their debut, the second album again paid tribute to those who had inspired them. On the back cover, the band printed Primo Levi's poem 'Song Of Those Who Died In Vain'.

Levi is an understandable hero for the band. As one of the greatest writers and literary historians of the Holocaust, his prose and poetry continues to inspire. A chemistry graduate, Levi was born in Turin in 1919. In 1943 he joined a partisan group in Northern Italy, where he was arrested and later transported to Auschwitz. His profession saved him from the gas chambers, and he was liberated with the rest of his camp at the end of the war. On his return to Italy he continued to work as a chemist, and write, until he retired. On April 11, 1987, Levi committed suicide by throwing himself down a stairwell in the home in which in was born. It is not known whether he killed himself because he was "ashamed" to have survived the Holocaust when so many others died, or whether he was simply weighted down with personal concerns.

"We, the survivors, are not the true witnesses," Levi once said. The real witnesses were those who had drowned, been submerged or annihilated – not just destroyed but completely wiped from existence. Levi felt that he was merely writing by proxy on behalf of them, and in 'The Drowned And The Saved' he tells us that there is always a dark, evil side to human nature and that we need to learn from the past.

Richey responded strongly to Levi's themes and was outraged whenever Revisionist historians attempted to play down Nazi atrocities, or even simply deny them.

"And yet within a few decades, you've got books being written, saying the Holocaust was a lie, which are getting some kind of academic credence now. And that's really, really offensive. And dangerous" (Richey, Melody Maker).

There is a case to be argued that in highlighting authors like Levi, the Manics were also expressing our need to learn from history. The album was released at a time when music and politics' intertwining was particularly tight. The topics of war veterans ('La Tristesse Durera'), narcotics ('Drug Drug Druggy') and mental illness, all of which 'Gold Against The Soul' covered, sat comfortably during a period of analysis. "There's nothing nice in my head, the adult world took it all away," wrote Richey ('From Despair To Where').

The band have always proclaimed their admiration for Public Enemy (another politically subversive band signed to the same label) and bands of their ilk, so it was maybe not so surprising that they chose to undertake a tour in July 1993 with Blaggers ITA and Credit To The Nation. James saw it as a way to stop complacency, declaring how much he was impressed by the "violent threat" of the Blaggers' live shows. At the same time that 'La Tristesse Durera' was released, Nicky

made another statement to go down in Manic history. In professing that he thought upper-class drop-outs who become travellers should be treated more ruthlessly, he ranted, "I wouldn't care if they were rounded up and put on an island."

"I don't think they perform any worthwhile role in society," he added (NME).

As always, Richey soon jumped to his bandmate's defence.

"We always open our mouths before we think. But that's part of where we come from, part of having fuck-all to do all day and saying things to each other simply to create argument" (Richey, NME).

After a support slot with Bon Jovi and another single ('Roses In The Hospital'), Wire was, as ever, able to laugh at himself. "I do consider myself to be something of a pretentious wanker," he informed Kerrang!

Sadly, the band were soon to receive some catastrophic news. After a two-year battle against cancer, Philip Hall, the band's publicist, co-manager and mentor, died on December 7, 1993. Hall, who was well-liked in the industry and respected for his unassuming nature, had also worked with The Pogues, The Stone Roses, The Waterboys, The Beautiful South and Radiohead, as well as cultivating The Manics from the bleakness of Blackwood to their current success. Hall always went beyond the call of duty with his bands; he was part of the family.

"We lived with him for virtually a year, he lent us about £45,000 before we got a deal, virtually financed us," Nicky explained to the NME. It was not surprising that the band were devastated, and they were poignant in expressing the grief they felt at the loss:

"He had a big impact on our lives. He was the first person that ever believed in our music, the first to respond to all the stupidly long letters we would send out to anyone we could think of. He said, 'I'll come and see you do a gig in London'. We said we couldn't get a gig in London. So he drove down to see us rehearse in a crappy schoolroom. Before we had a record deal, he'd only recently been married, and he told us, 'You've got no money, you can live with us.' We stayed with him for a year, sleeping in two spare bedrooms, the kitchen and the lounge" (Richey, Melody Maker).

"Philip was the first person who understood us. He was more than a manager, and his input into the band was invaluable. Without his help, motivation and generosity, it is doubtful whether we, as a band, would have carried on" (Manic Street Preachers' statement to the NME).

Out of respect to Philip, the band cancelled their gig at London's Brixton Academy. In March, they played a benefit gig for Cancer Research, with former Suede guitarist Bernard Butler guesting on 'Motorcycle Emptiness' and a cover of The Faces' 'Stay With Me'. A year later, Nicky said that the death of their friend and manager had affected them very deeply and that cutting themselves off by going on tour in January 1994 was a mechanism for blocking it out. Wire told Melody Maker that the band were reaching another point of change, and he quoted Henry Miller to explain their moves further: "At the edge of eternity is torture, in our mind's never-ending ambition to damage itself."

It was a huge clue for what was coming, in the shape of 'The Holy Bible'.

"It's a period of readjustment for us as people and as a band. We've reached some sort of conclusion in our career, and the question is, what next? And what we want to do next is very dark and very depressing" (Nicky, Melody Maker).

The new year began with another single, 'Life's Becoming A Landslide', and the music press screamed, "It's 1994 and the Manic Street Preachers are the only band that matters" (Melody Maker). Nothing appeared to be hidden any more, and through the press, which Richey seemed to use at times like a confessional, their fans heard souls being bared.

Once more, the subject of Richey's drink-dependency came up. "I am paranoid about not being able to sleep," he told Melody Maker.

"...And if by about eight o'clock at night I haven't had a drink, I get massive panic attacks, and I'll be awake all night, and that's my biggest nightmare. I can't stomach that thought. That's why I drink... My need is... functional. By about midday, I need a drink to stabilise me, but I've got to drive to the group rehearsal, so I can't have that drink. But on tour, I drink all day, just so I don't have to think about going on stage. That's why, as a live band, we fuck up so many times."

"The hero of yesterday becomes the tyrant of tomorrow, unless he crucifies himself today" (Joseph Campbell).

In Seattle, on Tuesday April 5, 1994, Kurt Cobain walked into his garage, took a large dose of heroin, wrote a letter saying that it was better to "burn out than fade away", laid out the letter and some personal belongings, and shot himself through the head with a shotgun. As Cobain's suicide sent shockwaves through the music world, Nicky commented, "I find the idea of him taking his own life frighteningly powerful... I've always been a sucker for that" (NME).

For Richey, though, there had just been too many demises. The month before, his best friend from university, whom he had shared a flat with, had hung himself.

"That threw Richey, seemed to affect him an awful lot, 'cos he never made many friends, and that was one of them" (Nicky, VOX).

Often paralleled with Nirvana, the Manics shared several similarities with the Seattle band. The Manics' views on sexuality had always been given prominence. Both bands had no gender division in their fans, and both had been known to don women's clothes in their time. For the Manics especially, their androgyny – wearing make-up, using slogans like 'All rock'n'roll is homosexual', sleeping with groupies, their views on sex and relationships – has on the one hand added to the confusion and on the other made their views very blatant. Perhaps that goes some way to explain their incredibly broad appeal. On a sold-out trip to Bangkok, the same seediness that Richey exposed in his diary for Select when walking around London's Soho district came out again. The area was described as an "HIV supermarket". "You find yourself leaving most of your Western

I know
I believe
in nothing
but it is
my nothing

ideas/ideals at the airport when you arrive," James told Raw.

For Bradfield, the visit had turned him into a complete 'lad', and at the time he expressed his thoughts about women as that of "slight irreverence".

"I don't feel any need to be accepted by women whatsoever, which is the way I've always felt, so it's reassuring to be me for once" (James, NME).

Later in the year, the band discussed, with trademark candour, their feelings on pornography and the sex industry. James and Richey could see no harm in soft porn as an aid through "rites of passage".

"It's helped me through fallow periods. Everyone goes through a dodgy period when they can't pull anything. Porn just gives you a quick relief. It just sends you to sleep, really... Men just want to see women with their legs open" (James, Select).

Having once said that he thought sex was just "an iota removed from a wank", Richey did say that he didn't want to be photographed naked in the porn magazine For Women, which they had been asked to do. His reasons? Primarily because his tackle was "too small".

For Richey, known for not having any long-term relationships, the visit to Bangkok was memorable for two reasons. A journalist who went with them was amazed by the dichotomy: one moment he had been incredibly eloquent and knowledgeable, discussing how developing economies, such as Thailand, abused their young; he later went off to a brothel and bought himself a hand job from a prostitute. "Perhaps... I don't regard paying for sex as being that different to sleeping with a groupie. It's all done on the same functional level," Richey explained (NME), saying the experience "just passed a few hours" (Raw).

He also felt that he wasn't a very sexual person, and was afraid of becoming involved with anyone, saying, "I don't feel strong enough to cope with the rejection if they left me" (Select). It was a fear he put into his lyrics ("My idea of love comes from a childhood glimpse of pornography" from 'Life Becoming A Landslide').

The second reason was that on the same trip, where the band played to around 8,000 people

"When I cut myself I feel so much better. All the little things that might ha

in just two nights, the issue of Richey's self-harm was again brought to the fore. Richey had been given a set of knives by a Thai fan. Although he said that he wasn't going to be "anyone's circus sideshow freak" (Select), it was noticeable that Richey's torso was bleeding as he took the stage.

Twenty years before, Iggy Pop, while on tour with The Stooges, had also slashed himself on stage with bottles, but was this the same thing? What kind of pressure are these very visual people under to publicly lacerate themselves? Richey James, part case study, part psychoanalyst, described his needs quite rationally:

"When I cut myself I feel so much better. All the little things that might have been annoying me suddenly seem so trivial because I'm concentrating on the pain. I'm not a person who can scream and shout, so this is my only outlet. It's all done very logically" (NME).

Perhaps to justify himself, he also claimed to see philosophical dimensions.

"I think people are becoming more machine-like and that's the imagery I like. Also sex and death are closely linked. Sado-masochistic imagery, bleeding... I find it attractive. I find it... sexual" (Richey, Select).

It then becomes all the more apparent why lyrics such as "Stub cigarettes out on my arm" ('Roses In The Hospital') and "I am an architect, they call me a butcher" ('Faster') can be read as such very personal songs. When the band played the latter on Top Of The Pops, their terrorist-style clothing caused a flurry of complaints. Nicky explained further that 'Faster' was a "...voyeuristic insight into how our generation has become obliterated with sensations. We could deal with things, but we prefer to blank them out so that virtually every atrocity doesn't have that much impact any more" (NME).

Despite tales stretching as far back as The Bible, in which Jesus is said to have met a hermit who cut himself with knives, public recognition of self-harm has been slow not only in the medical world but also in society, which has chosen to hide it away with other taboo areas. Psychiatry only officially recognised its existence in the '60s, and as far as the law is concerned, although self-harm is not a criminal offence, under the 1983 Mental Health Act, those who commit the act in a public place can be arrested and detained for up to 72 hours in a place of safety. In addition, concerned friends and family are also able to solicit a social worker's advice if someone self-harms in their own home.

The theories behind such behaviour are inconclusive. Whether it is an obsessive-compulsive disorder, caused by disturbances in the brain's neuro-transmitters, a genetic predisposition, or connected to the body's natural painkillers (endorphines), no views are absolute. However, what is more certain is that self-harmers are not trying to commit suicide; it is an action which can be seen as a release mechanism or as self-control. It is more about survival than suicide, and many self-harmers claim that if they didn't hurt themselves, they may do worse things. Although many have depressive symptoms and have low self-esteem, they are not all clinically depressed, so treatment with anti-depressives is not always appropriate.

A high proportion of self-harmers are women, and around 75 per cent of those have been sexually abused. One of the few helplines available is run by the Bristol Crisis Service For Women. However, The Barnes Unit at John Radcliff Hospital, Oxford, which specialises in treatment of self-harmers, found that one of the highest proportions demographically is the 20- to 24-year-old male group. Hospital admittance of patients who have self-harmed is around 100,000 a year, of these it is estimated that 15,000 cut themselves. Statistics are not precise; such casualties may be counted under another medical remit, and many don't end up going to hospital at all.

been annoying me suddenly seem so trivial."

In many ways, self-harming underscores the tribal nature of youth culture. Talking about punk rock, Dick Hebdige explained that he saw its very visual culture and the accompanying assaults on the body (tattoos and piercing) as a sign-system. When Sid Vicious ground broken glass into his chest, he seemed to be saying that, if nothing else, young people owned their bodies, and self-mutilation was a way of exercising power over it:

"It can be cut up and cooked like a piece of meat. Self-mutilation is just the darker side of narcissism. The body becomes the base-line, the place where the buck stops."

Richey's views were somewhat similar.

"[It's] like when the air is really muggy and a good thunderstorm clears the air. That's the best analogy I can think of" (Richey, Raw).

During May, the Manics played second headline at a huge anti-Nazi carnival at Brockwell Park, south London, with around 130,000 people attending. In spite of earlier rantings that political correctness was one of the greatest evils of our time, Richey says that the gig was "above politics... just a central part of being a good human being" (NME).

A few weeks later, at another enormous outdoor gig at Glastonbury, Nicky proved that he hadn't lost his touch for winding people up by pronouncing that they should "build some more by-passes over this shithole".

As each Manic-event is added to their history, and especially since the notorious '4 REAL' incident, it has to be wondered whether the public had become more and more hardened to each move that the band in general, and Richey, in particular, made. What motivated someone who didn't know him to offer him knives to cut himself with?

Whatever the answer, and there can be no simple one, the band were about to push their limits on all levels again.

"All the best bands get really fucked up... we're not saying there's anything glamorous in getting fucked up, we're not saying there's anything glamorous in being dead, but there's nothing glamorous in having a 20-year career in rock either. That's even more sick" (Nicky, Melody Maker).

"We're not saying there's anything glamorous in being dead, but there's

THE AGE OF (IN) REA
THE AGE OF (IN) REASON
THE AGE OF (IN)

ASON (IN) REASON
THE AGE OF (IN) REASON
THE AGE OF (IN) REASON
THE AGE OF (IN) REASON
THE AGE OF (IN) REASON

nothing glamorous in having a 20-year career in rock, either."

THE AGE OF ENLIGHTENMENT

THE AGE OF ENLIGHTENMENT

THE AGE OF ENLIGHTENMENT

ENLIGHTENMENT

THE AGE OF ENLIGHTENMENT

E OF ENLIGHTENMENT

THE AGE OF ENLIGHTENMENT

THE AGE OF ENLIGHTENMENT

AGE OF ENLIGHTENMENT

OR ENLIGHTENMENT

THE AGE OF ENLIGHTENMENT

THE AGE OF ENLIGHTENMENT

THE AGE OF ENLIGHTENMENT

"The hero of yesterday becomes the tyrant of tomorrow, unless he crucifies himself today..."

THE AGE OF ENLIGHTENMENT

BY AUGUST 1994, the inevitable had happened. Following rumours of a two-day self-mutilation spree (which was strongly denied at the time by the band's management) at his home in Cardiff during July, as well as a piece in Melody Maker saying that he had threatened to quit the band, Richey finally admitted that he needed help. He was taken to a psychiatric clinic, where he was treated for 'nervous exhaustion', a catch-all phrase which can include a number of physical and mental symptoms, such as insomnia, aching, loss of energy and depression. For Richey, it meant alcoholism, anorexia and self-harm.

"For the first time I was a bit scared, because I always thought I could handle it. I've read lots of books about tolerance of pain and pain thresholds. The euphoric agony, basically, is a sensation which your mind blocks off. You control yourself. It's all about control. About proving a point to yourself, which I did very easily but then I realised I couldn't do anything. So I went to hospital" (Richey, VOX).

The "artistic abyss" he'd walked past for so long had become the void he had fallen into, according to Nicky. After admittance to Whitchurch, an NHS hospital in Cardiff, where he stayed for eight days, Richey was then moved to a private clinic – The Priory in Roehampton, London – which was found for him by the band's manager, Martin Hall. By all accounts, Whitchurch had been a nightmare: Richey had been placed on a ward with around a dozen other men and dosed up with anti-depressants. It was hardly conducive to a speedy recovery.

The private, £300-a-day Priory hospital, has many specialist programmes, including an eating disorders unit, an anorexia clinic and the Galsworthy Lodge addiction unit. Spending three months there, Richey undertook the 12-Step recovery programme, the same treatment taken by Shaun Ryder. Based on the same steps used by Alcoholics Anonymous, the programme was originally designed for recovering alcoholics.

"The programme is designed to help people face the reality of their dependency and to promote the restoration of physical and emotional help through abstinence and continuing support" (Priory Hospital leaflet).

The main objectives are for addicts to admit that they are powerless over their addiction and that their lives have become unmanageable. It suggests they reconcile themselves with a 'God of their understanding'. For Shaun Ryder, this meant an image of his grandmother, but Richey couldn't find a similar image because he was scared that "they would die". Later, James likened the experience not to One Flew Over The Cuckoo's Nest (one of their favourite films) but to a floatation tank, which kept Richey in limbo.

Explaining their friend's vulnerability James and Nicky said respectively:

"There's a trigger in Richey that he can't control. He doesn't have a second skin. He has a mental illness... You can do all you can, but you can't put someone in a strait-jacket. It's a cliché, but you can only be there for the fall" (James, Rapid Mood Swings).

"[To my mind] The Priory ripped out the man and left a shell. These people say they've got a cure, but that cure is to totally change your personality. And you could see him struggling with this, wondering if this was the only way..." (Nicky, Select).

For James, it was the culmination of a series of events that had dragged his friend down into an abyss of despair and despondency.

"I was probably much more worried about Richey at other points that this year. Like when we recorded the first album; he was royally fucked-up then in terms of every kind of abuse. He would cry a lot. But it always got back on an even keel quite easily. Then, this last Christmas, I felt he

was the oldest and yet the youngest of us all. He'd only experience things by forcing himself into situations. He was quite immature in terms of what he'd experienced in life, never been in a relationship, things like that. So perhaps then I realised that he definitely was beginning to feel emptier. No matter what I said, there was nothing I could do to make him feel better. But it's still a surprise when something happens" (James, NME).

Nicky and Richey had earlier been nicknamed 'The Glamour Twins', but Nicky began pointing out that they weren't exactly alike. "Richey was black and I was white," he said on a later press release.

"The difference between me and Richey is he always wanted to be understood, and I prefer being misunderstood. I don't feel the need for people to love or respect me, whereas Richey really did" (Nicky, Rapid Mood Swings).

The band were at a low ebb and they were all feeling it. In an interview with Melody Maker, Nicky spoke freely about himself, and in hindsight, about Richey, too.

"Richey always wanted to be understood..."

"All I can remember is being melancholy," he said. "I've never said I was desperately unhappy. The truly unhappy people of this world are usually the ones who end up suicidal or living on the streets."

He also said that although he believed Richey was very sensitive – he just took too much in – there was no doubt in his mind that being in a band had exacerbated his problems.

"It was obvious that he had to go to hospital. There was no other option. He realised it, his parents realised it. He's just really ill, in a lot of ways, at the moment. I don't want to get maudlin about it, but obviously something's gone a bit awry" (NME).

While Richey was battling with himself, the rest of the Manics played two of the big summer festivals as a three-piece. Strathclyde's T-In-The-Park was certainly seen as a very different gig without Richey. "Close your eyes and nothing's changed, but look up there and there's an empty space and something feels very wrong indeed," wrote the NME. They also played as a trio at Reading (on what would have been Philip Hall's birthday). Nicky said the show "felt like a betrayal" and that it was "terrible" without Richey (Select). However, although it was difficult, they didn't want to let their fans down.

As far as the future of the band was concerned, Nicky told one paper that without Richey the Manics would not continue, "in any shape or form" (Rapid Mood Swings); he told the Daily Mirror that Richey was "definitely not going to leave", and said as much to the NME:

"Basically, the way we see it is that he'll be back as quick as possible, and if it ever comes to the point where he's not coming back we won't continue" (NME).

Amid rumours of a split, Hall Or Nothing, the Manics' PR company, sent out a statement to the press saying that Richey was suffering from mental illness and that there had been no change in his condition:

"Speculation that Richey is leaving the group is completely unfounded. Even from the clinic he is still very much involved with the artwork and other aspects of the new album. He is, however, very ill at the moment, and things have now developed to a point where the band – but more importantly Richey – have decided that he needs to seek professional psychiatric help to deal with what is basically a sickness."

"To be honest, we were all quite numb to any sort of discussion about the group's future because we were too concerned about Richey," James told Q. "We've all grown up together. He's a friend first and foremost. So we never entertained any discussion about the group until he brought it up himself... it would have been a betrayal."

Richey confided in James that he had wanted to cut himself again on the last tour, and Bradfield had reassured him that he had the support to leave whenever he wanted. Deep down, however, this wasn't what James wanted. "If he left, the band would probably be over. I can't imagine the Manics without him," he told The Times.

James no longer felt comfortable to go on living out the rock'n'roll cliché. "Some things will have to change, but that's OK. I'll have to find a new drinking buddy," James told Q. For the sake of his friend's health, it was time to do things differently. By this time, Richey had also joined Alcoholics Anonymous, and just as his character was being dissected and assessed inside the hospital, so it was being analysed by everyone outside.

His friends in the band tried to make sense of it all.

"Everyone's got a corner of their heart and mind you can't get into. Richey was always much more into books and films than rock'n'roll, and I think those art forms are much more idealised. I think they influenced the way he viewed his life, and the way he thought it would be. Whenever I talk about Richey, I think of that quote from Rumblefish, y'know? He's merely miscast to play; he was born on the wrong side of the river. He has the ability to do anything but he can't find anything he wants to do" (James, The Times).

His friends were just as concerned:

"The thing is, he doesn't see anything wrong in cutting himself. It makes him feel better. It's his way of releasing pain, and his argument is, it doesn't harm anyone else. It's almost like a badge to show he's emotionally strong enough to deal with problems in his own way. He was at the point, though, where no one – not even himself – knew how far he might go. If he had carried on without any help he might have ended up killing himself" (Martin Hall, Select).

The media was also trying to understand:

Revol.
Mr Lenin - awaken the boy. Mr Stalin -
bi-sexual epoch. Kruschev - self love
in his mirrors. Breshnev - married into
group sex. Gorbachev - celibate self-importance.
Yeltsin - failure is his own impotence. revol - revol.
revol - revol. lebensraum - Kulturkampf - raus -
raus - fila - fila. Napoleon - childhood sweethearts.
Chamberlain - you see God in you. Trotsky -
honeymoon, serenade the naked. Che Guevara -
you're all target now. Pol Pot - withdrawn traces,
bye bye. Farrakhan - alimony alimony.
revol - revol. revol - revol. lebensraum -
Kulturkampf - raus - raus - fila - fila. revol -
revol. revol - revol. lebensraum - Kulturkampf -
raus - raus - fila - fila. revol.

"I would like to be able to write, "I'm feeling supersonic, give me a gin and tonic", but I just can't do it. I think that it's a brilliant lyric..."

"I don't hold with the 'cry for help' theories. There's nothing exhibitionist about it. Richey cuts and bleeds and... cuts some more at home, alone. Armchair shrinks might speculate that Richey's razor scars and anorexia reflect a wish to keep some vestigial level of control over his life. But fuck psychoanalysis. The nation's mental hospitals are filled with unrecognised clairvoyants, misunderstood seers. I've known more than one. Depression is a sickness; too sensitive for this world Richey may be, but he is not insane" (Simon Price, Melody Maker).

Price, a long-time fan of the band, spoke with tenderness. He later said that what set Richey apart from others was his ability to "articulate the horror". This was not true of some other journalists, who had already started to dig a premature plot for Richey, next to Kurt Cobain.

Later, and uncharacteristically, Richey chose not to discuss much of his time in the clinic:

"There has to be some kind of privacy. Inevitably I'm bound to be misrepresented, but that's something that everybody has to deal with" (Time Out).

Genius or madman? That was the running dichotomy in the debate. However, the band's management were confident that he would be fit for the autumn tour, and although they didn't take him any press reports, they did keep in daily contact with him, taking in the album's artwork for approval. James told Raw that his friend demanded flawlessness of himself when it came to putting together the words and sleeve of the new album:

"Richey has always been in love with rose-tinted perfection, so he was always in danger of being let down and something like this happening."

The band were often asked if Richey's health was symptomatic of the pressures of the industry:

"I don't think of it as a natural extension of being in a rock group. It might have accelerated it, but that's all. In some ways Richey's a very Richard Briers person – very cardigan, pipe and slippers. But I think if he'd gone on to become a lecturer – which he might well have done – the same thing could have very easily happened, perhaps in a more private way" (James, Q).

On August 30, the band released 'The Holy Bible', their third album, which they dedicated to Philip Hall. It was not the most uplifting or listener-friendly of records, and it remains one of their most formidable to date. "It's not a party record," James told Raw. "It's not 'Abba Gold', but there are a few basic home truths on it."

In terms of subject matter, the album was very grim indeed. There were two tracks about the Holocaust ('Mausoleum' and 'Intense Humming of Evil'); 'Archives of Pain', which used French philosopher Michael Foucault's study of punishment as a reference point, was about the cult and glorification of serial killers; the self-explanatory 'Die in the Summertime'

"In some ways, Richey is a very Richard Briers person."

("Scratch my leg with a rusty nail/Sadly it heals") looked at death; and the much-analysed '4st 7lb', took on anorexia ("I want to walk in the snow and not leave a footprint"). The album also dealt with dictatorship ('Of Walking Abortion'), American gun laws ('Ifwhiteamericatoldthetruthforonedayitsworldwould-fallapart'), relationships and sexual desire ('Revol' and 'She Is Suffering' respectively).

James felt the album was "...lyrically, far more potent; musically, a lot more stripped down. It was recorded in a really shit studio in the red-light district in Cardiff. It was really bleak, seedy and perfectly suited" (Volume).

The split in lyric-writing had altered; Richey had written about three-quarters of the words for this, their most bleak work. The band had visited Dachau, Belsen and Hiroshima's Peace Museum the previous year, and it had affected them quite profoundly. It made them realise how history

has been manipulated – for example, the widespread belief that America had to drop the bomb in order to stop the Second World War. Nicky told Melody Maker that he was perturbed about the "human capacity to inflict pain on its own race", and that it was this that they were writing about. When 'Of Walking Abortion' questions who is responsible for all the atrocities, the answer howls back, "You fucking are..."

"It's as if they've peered into the abyss for so long, they can see nothing but the abyss peering back at them," said Andy Gill (The Independent). They had also entered those parts of the human psyche that most bands have qualms about touching, for fear of contamination. After Richey's disappearance, Caitlin Moran took the point further, in relation to 'The Holy Bible':

"Just as a woman's body irrevocably changes shape after she has had a child, so I now believe that musicians' heads warp and bend after certain songs have been in there" (The Times).

The opening track, 'Yes', was a very reflective look at the way the band felt they had prostituted themselves. One line in it – "There's no part of my body that has not been used" – Nicky likened to "...what Red Indians believe, that your soul is taken away when you're photographed constantly. It does get to a point where it feels like that" (NME). For Richey, the song was also autobiographical; "I hurt myself to get pain out," cries Bradfield.

Overall, Nicky felt the album revealed the state of depression they were experiencing, and Richey explained that he didn't feel the band had ever made happy records.

"I would like to be able to write "I'm feeling supersonic, give me gin and tonic", but I just can't do it. I think that it's a brilliant lyric, but whatever ability that is, I haven't got the ability to write that line. I don't feel that way, you know?" (NME).

The album went on to sell over 75,000 in the UK, but in the press, initial reviews kept a close eye on the private side of the band. In a particularly prophetic piece, Simon Williams said that it was a "vile" record which reminded him of Nirvana's 'In

Utero'. "Remember what happened next?" he warned NME. Upbeat in pace and depressing in sentiment, it also recalled early Joy Division, circa 'Unknown Pleasures'. It made an interesting analogy which would grow with the band.

The album's cover was also up for debate. In the same way they used language as their weapon, as a band they had also understood how an image can "shock and inspire". The front cover was a triptych of a large woman in her underwear, painted by Jenny Saville, which Richey had seen in a magazine; it was the complete antithesis of the anorexic subject of '4st 7lbs'. When the painting went on display, with a £30,000 price tag, at the Saatchi art gallery, Richey talked to the artist. Whatever he said, it was convincing, and Saville said they could use it for nothing. The band were accused of making a derogatory statement about women and body image, but Richey countered this with an extremely well-versed and knowledgeable understanding of feminism and censorship debates, using ideas from as far afield as Andrea Dworkin and Brett Easton Ellis' novel American Psycho. Richey, with a philosophy or quote for every question, said he failed to understand how some people could find The Sun offensive and yet were quite happy to read De Sade's 120 Days of Sodom.

At the Blue Stone Studio, in Pembrokeshire, Richey had made a return, and Stuart Bailie went along to interview the band for NME. Richey was looking forward to a short tour of France, supporting Therapy?. Like some kind of confessional, he began to put together the pieces of himself that had fallen apart over the last few years. Always self-effacing, he explained how he had positioned himself in the world. It helps to explain the subject matter of the album:

"I'm a melodramatic drama queen. I can't help that. Everything I've ever liked in literature, especially, has been along those lines. I guess I identify with victims, but that's just the way I am. Everything I've ever studied in my life, at university I specialised in the Holocaust and Nazi/Soviet foreign policy. That's what I did" (NME).

Again, the issue of sleep, or lack of it, came up, and how he was frightened of sleep because of "the things I get in my head". He explained that this was the reason he had begun drinking. Now, Richey had turned to exercise to keep the figure he had sought through his eating disorder. Having confessed to being vain, Richey was now doing 1,500 sit-ups a day to retain a flat stomach. In one of the most frank interviews he had ever given, quoted in some length below,

"The last thing I wanted to do was end up a fucking junkie alcoholic mess..."

Richey talked very lucidly and compassionately about the abuse he had been putting his body through with alcohol and self-harm.

"The last thing I wanted to do was end up a fucking junkie alcoholic mess like Shane MacGowan... The thing about self-harm is that you are aware of what you're doing. That's how you justify it... It's the arbitrary factors that determine your life. That's a certain kind of beauty in taking complete control of every aspect of your life. Purifying or hurting your body to achieve a balance in your mind is tremendously disciplined...

"You just get to a point where if you don't do it to yourself, you get a feeling that something really terrible is going to happen, and when that moment comes, it's the logical thing to do. It doesn't hurt. You're not screaming and shouting. A couple of days later you feel like a sad fuck, but that's part of the healing process; after that you feel really good. People that harm themselves, be it through anorexia or razors, know what they're doing" (Time Out).

Some of their most fantastic live shows came after the terrible events of the summer. By Christmas they had toured with Suede in Europe and played three stunning sell-out shows at the Astoria in London on December 19, 20 and 21. The Astoria shows were incredible, the band hurling round their equipment, trashing the lot at the cost of a mere £10,000.

Until that point they had been happier to demolish cheaper gear but at the London show, according to Sean, "it was almost as if we were trying to destroy everything so we could never play another gig" (Select).

"If 1994 was The Year Rock Cracked Up, then it was the Manic Street Preachers who were wielding the sledgehammer," claimed a review of the London shows in the NME. Eighteen months later, Nicky pointed to this as the period when he wrote 'Further Away', which was to appear on their fourth album.

"And when I wrote it, on the Suede tour in 1994, I was aware that, for the first time ever in my life, I was starting to grow away from Richey. He came out of The Priory, full of this 12-point recovery programme and all that shit, and he just wasn't the same person any more as far as I was concerned." (Nicky, Melody Maker).

Of the Astoria shows, Wire said later that he felt that, as they smashed up their equipment, it really was the end of something. A new era was approaching. "We'll never be that good again," he told Melody Maker. "We had to change."

Richey gave Nicky a folder of around 60 of his lyrics, which he later copied and gave to the others. No questions were asked, and there were no clues as to what would happen next. By Christmas Day, Richey had stopped drinking, and when he ate a bar of chocolate, his family and friends felt that he had gone one step further in beating his eating disorder.

The following January, James was making it clear that although 1994 had been a "bag of shit", and although they'd "lost the plot a bit", they were now "back to speaking in tongues" (Select).

Normal service was about to be

resumed. The Manics had begun rehearsing at The House In The Wood studio in Surrey; Richey had finally moved away from home and bought his own flat in Cardiff; and both Nicky and Sean were living with their partners. Their next move was feverishly anticipated, and when Mark Sutherland reviewed their next London gig, he wasn't making an understatement when he said that, as a band, they brought with them "more baggage... than Ivana Trump on a months' Interrailing holiday." (NME).

Just as the band were undergoing negotiations for a deal to write the theme to Sylvester Stallone's new sci-fi blockbuster Judge Dredd, Richey was interviewed on January 23, 1995, by Midori Tsukagoshi, for the Japanese magazine Music Life. It is very easy, with hindsight, to go back and look for clues, but to all intents and purposes, was the fact that Richey had shaved off all his hair, or that he was wearing striped pyjamas (eerily reminiscent of outfits worn by the inmates of Auschwitz), so very important compared to the events of the previous year?

Richey told Tsukagoshi that he couldn't sleep, and that to avoid any "destructive ideas" he had shaved his head and tossed away loads of his notebooks of lyrics into a river outside his home. He agreed that being hospitalised he had "got lost somewhere", because at times he was "just fed up with myself". He went on to say that his pet dog had died, and how upset he was.

"You know, I miss my dog, Snoopy. He died two weeks ago. That's why I shaved my head... he was 17 years old. I've had him since I was little" (Music Life).

It was, as always with Richey James, an interview of some intellect. He conversed with some wisdom about his respect for the Japanese author Yukio Mishima (a quasi-fascist and masochist who committed ritual suicide in 1970 after an attempted right-wing coup had failed). Notably, he also spoke of his feelings for a woman. Having only been involved in one relationship since the band begun, he explained that he had only kissed the unnamed woman a couple of times, even though he'd known her for many years. It wasn't realistic to be in love, he explained, having written the word across his fingers that day.

This was to be Richey James' last known interview to date.

Nine days later he had disappeared.

"You know, I miss my dog, Snoopy. He died two weeks ago. That's why I shaved my head..."

CHAPTER FIVE

APOCALYPSE NOW

"**I**T WAS in the last six months that he really deteriorated. I could feel something was wrong. He'd call me late at night and talk about Apocalypse Now or Naked for two hours, trying to get some sort of idea across, and he just couldn't" (Nicky, The Guardian).

The music industry has embraced many tragedies, and most of them have been glamorised or mythologised. What follows is an account of the known details and events which occurred from February 1, 1995, onwards. Where there is any doubt over a piece of information it has been noted. To reiterate, no one apart from Richey himself knows what happened...

On the eve of an American tour, 28-year-old Richey was last seen leaving the London Embassy Hotel in Bayswater, London, on February 1, 1995, at 7am. The following day, Martin Hall reported Richey's disappearance to the Harrow Road Police Station in London W9.

On February 2, the details were compiled in the missing persons document number 584(C) with the case number: REF:584-21-DR-95.

Richard and James had booked into the hotel in the evening of January 31 as a stop-over before they flew out for a promotional visit to the States, a trip which was to include a 36-date tour beginning at Tucson, Arizona, on February 22 and ending at Phoenix, Arizona, on April 9. They had been given adjacent rooms and James said he would give Richey a knock after they'd freshened up. Half an hour later, James knocked and Richey answered, smiling. He was taking a bath, and when Bradfield asked if he wanted to go to Queensway, Richey replied that he was

"It was in the last six months that he really deteriorated. I could feel something was wrong."

thinking about going to the cinema. James wanted to go, too, so he planned to come back in half an hour's time. Around 8.30pm Richey told James that he was going to stay in and would see him in the morning. Bradfield went to meet a friend and returned at 11.30pm.

That was the last time James saw Richey. The next morning, his room was empty. On his bed was a parcel containing some books, a couple of videos (Equus and Naked), a photograph, some collages and a note, believed to be for an American woman, which read, 'I love you'. It has since been passed on to a 19-year-old woman called 'Jo', who it is thought it was intended for.

Richey went back to his Cardiff flat the same day, driving his silver Vauxhall Cavalier, registration number L519 HKX. At his home, he left some documents, including his passport, credit cards and the anti-depressant, Prozac.

The band's management company hired a private investigator, who discovered that Richey had withdrawn £2,000 from his account over the ten-day period prior to his disappearance, £200 each time until January 31. The account has not been touched since. The police report noted that Richey had previously attempted suicide and was taking anti-depressants.

Martin Hall, who raised the alarm by phoning the police, drove to Cardiff and searched inside the flat with Graham Edwards, Richey's father.

"There were no signs of Edwards or any note left to indicate he may have harmed himself" (Police report, quoted in VOX).

The Cavalier was identified by Avon and Somerset Officers at Aust service station, near the Severn Bridge. It was spotted by an attendant, who had noticed that it had been parked on the same spot since February 14. The car was traced by the police's national computer and confirmed to be Richey's, but despite extensive enquiries, no one at the service station

remembered seeing the driver. Tom Cassidy, the service station manager, said that the car was locked and that there was no note or package that made them suspicious. Graham Edwards picked up the Cavalier and drove it back to his home. The car's battery had been found flat, so it was thought that Richey had been sleeping rough in the car, probably playing tapes.

Police searched the area, known as a local suicide spot, and the coastal authorities were contacted to see if any bodies had been found washed up on the Bristol Channel shoreline. Nothing was found, although the strong tides and powerful undercurrent make suicide a sad possibility. However, Detective Frank Stockham, one of the officers involved with the case, said that owing to a nearby junction, where the M4 meets the M5, they had not ruled out the chance that he may have hitched a ride somewhere. A Scotland Yard spokesperson said that finding the car had not "shed any light" on the case (Press Association).

The Edwards family, who had last seen Richey on January 23 and had received a phone call from him eight days later, placed a simple appeal in a personal column for three consecutive days, simply saying: "Richard, please make contact. Love, Mum, Dad and Rachel." Ceefax also broadcast news of the disappearance, with a quote from Nicky expressing his concern. The first the media and public knew of the case was on February 15, when the South Wales Police and the Metropolitan Police, who were liaising on the case, issued the following press release:

South Wales Police – press release
Wed 15 February 1995
Member of local pop group reported missing
Police are anxious to trace Richard James Edwards, aged 28 years, a member of the pop group Manic Street Preachers, who has been missing from the London area since Wednesday February 1, 1995, when he was seen leaving the London Embassy Hotel at 7am. It is known that on the same day he visited his home in the Cardiff area...
Richard's family, band members and friends are concerned for his safety and welfare and stress that no pressure would be put on him to return if he does not wish to. They stress that his privacy will be respected at all times.
Police are asking anyone who has seen Richard, knows of his whereabouts, or has seen his car, to contact them at Cardiff Central Police station on 0222 222111, and ask for the Crimedesk or CID office.
Should Richard himself hear or see this appeal, his family and friends are anxious for him to contact one of them or the police to let them know he is safe and well. They again wish to stress that Richard will not be urged to return or reveal his whereabouts if he does not wish to do so. Ends
PRO/JMW 12 noon

On the same day, Graham Edwards gave an interview to Red Dragon Radio in Cardiff, saying that his son had "disappeared into thin air". Nicky – who had even rung a Swansea hotel where a Richard Edwards was staying, only to find out it was a businessman of the same name – told the press, "If Richey does not want to come back, then that is fine. But we just want him to give us a call or send us a postcard."

On February 20 the band's management company decided to postpone the American tour, which was due to start a couple of days later, and on February 22 a spokesperson for the band told the Western Mail: "We are obviously concerned and are beginning to fear the worst. The band has ground to a standstill – everyone is so upset."

The next day, Graham Edwards urged anyone with any information to come forward, and the following month he told a local paper: "I suppose it was a gradual decline... and it was only in June that we realised there was something seriously wrong" (Western Mail).

A few days after that, Graham and Sherry Edwards both spoke to the Daily Mail. "Wherever Richey has been in the world he has always got in touch," said his mother. "Whether it was a quick telephone call or a postcard, we always knew how he was doing" (Daily Mail).

"Parents are often the very last people to get inside their child's brain," added Graham.

But if Richey was alive, what could anyone do? As the detective in charge of the case, Stephen Moray, pointed out – "Every adult has the right just to go missing" (The Times).

Journalists immediately ran to psychiatrists for 'expert' opinions, but the band and many close to them remained quiet, having made a conscious decision not to talk to the press. With good intentions, the music press continued to highlight events, hoping that publicity would bring more information and running helpline numbers to support mourning fans. Letters flooded into the music papers – the same music papers the band had once lived for, according to James Brown:

"The Manic Street Preachers live for interviews. Any time a tape recorder appears, they load up with venom and rhetoric and go for the throat" (NME).

"Wind 'em up, watch 'em go," was how Melody Maker's Simon Price described them. Now the press was being inundated with distraught fans, some of them sending in pictures of bleeding limbs. The band, who had previously received notes from other self-harmers looking for support, were now receiving letters written in blood. Melody Maker's Backlash page was swamped with letters from fans – some containing razors, asking the magazine to dispose of them on their behalf. Melody Maker implored anyone who had difficulty in dealing with Richey's disappearance to carry on writing, if it gave them an outlet. They also listed the numbers of helplines, including that of The Samaritans, with whom they later collaborated to make a charity record.

In April, the same paper ran two outstanding features. The first was a candid and explicit understanding of his own depression written by MM writer Andrew Mueller. The following week their cover featured a picture of Richey alongside another of Kurt Cobain, with the headline, 'From Despair To Where?' Inside, a poignant Samaritans advert carried the words to REM's 'Everybody Hurts', and a panel of readers, musicians, journalists and people from the music industry discussed a year in which depression and music took each other by the hand.

After Sally Allen, a 17-year-old school girl, went missing in Yorkshire on March 3, it was discovered that she had been a big Manics fan, and of Richey in particular. She had cut off her

"Parents are often the very last people to get inside their child's brain."

hair and lost a lot of weight. One letter to Melody Maker, from a woman called Jasmine, from Sunderland, was, sadly, not untypical:

"I cut Richey's name into my arm because I'm so depressed."

Richey was an icon, open about the dark side of human nature; someone who could speak so eloquently about self-harm on behalf of all those who had felt speechless.

Another fan wrote:

"Until I know that Richey is safe, I'll keep starving, I'll keep bingeing, I'll keep dyeing my hair, I'll keep cutting deeper and crying harder, and if there's anything left when Richey comes home, then I'll smile" (Melody Maker).

Not all of the letters were quite as desperate, although there was another, equally powerful letter, from Helen of Ashford, who said:

"It was Richey who first attracted me to the Manics. By chance, I stumbled across an interview he gave just after he came out of hospital. He seemed like such a nice person. At a time when I felt so alone and depressed, it was comforting to know that someone out there felt the same. He hasn't encouraged me to harm myself, but just made me feel less alone.

"Richey is a very special person who has touched many people with his lyrics and brave, honest interviews. I just hope he's OK" (Melody Maker).

It is understandable, then, that when the Harrow Road station was faxed the news that the body of a tattooed man had been washed up just off Beachy Head on July 21, the police were cautioned, "Please be aware before making public."

It was later confirmed that the body was not Richey's.

Raking over the past, the press began to pull out what they considered to be significant references to people taking their own lives. Tracks such as 'Suicide Alley' and 'Suicide is Painless', took on a new, morbid significance. Lyrics were dissected (eg: "Life is a slow suicide," from 'Motorcycle Emptiness'), and references the band had made were made into theses. It was noted that Richey had been fascinated by Tony Hancock's suicide note, which said, "Things just went wrong too many times..." Richey apparently once remarked, "I think that's one of the most beautiful things I've ever read" (NME).

Nicky could see why these points were being made.

"We were all attracted to the glamour of suicides and alcohol and beauty, that Rumblefish thing of self-destruction. It's just that Richey took it a lot further. Richey took things a lot further than us. Ian Curtis and Kurt Cobain were the two Richey icons. The Hendrixes and the rest were just decadent. But Kurt and Ian meant to do it – took control. That was more fascinating to Richey" (Select).

The band, and Richey in particular, often cited the Francis Ford Coppola film Apocalypse Now (1979) as a major influence. Loosely based on Joseph Conrad's novella Heart of Darkness, the film is a battle of good and evil, about sanity and the darker side of human nature. There are

underlying themes of degradation, suicide and rock'n'roll, with a soundtrack which includes The Doors' 'The End' and 'Satisfaction' by the Rolling Stones. Coppola said it was a film that would give the audience "a sense of the horror, the madness, the sensuousness and the moral dilemma of the Vietnam War."

In the film's opening shots, the camera whirls deliriously around the film's star, Martin Sheen, lying on an unmade bed. Seemlessly and wilfully, Sheen begins to lacerate himself on a mirror. Watching this now, there is undoubtedly a powerful connection between Sheen's improvised mutilations and Richey's '4 REAL' incident.

Every man has a breaking point, Apocalypse Now tells us as chaos and primal fear take over, and the last words express "the horror" of it all. Like the Manics themselves, the film is incredibly intense, dwelling on the rocky balance of sanity and madness. There are also strong parallels in terms of the media: where the film has journalists wanting to capture every, almost surreal, detail of the psychology of war, so the music press gathered every detail of Richey's mental configuration. Also, like the history of the band, Apocalypse Now was dogged by incredible hardships in its production. Way over budget, Coppola funded most of the film himself; a typhoon destroyed much of the set; Sheen had a heart attack; both Sheen and Coppola suffered breakdowns; and, to cap it all, there was a civil war going on in the Philippines where they were filming.

Richey, who had a framed picture of the film's poster in his living room, was evidently obsessed with the film, even wearing cameras around his neck like the photo-journalist in the film (played by Dennis Hopper), right down to the exact make and model.

"La tristesse durera" ("This sadness will go on"), the last words of Van Gogh, were often quoted by Richey, but many have ruled out the possibility of him taking his own life. Byron Harris told the NME that his friend never did anything without a reason, and others remembered Richey saying:

"In terms of the 'S' word, that does not enter my mind. And it never has done. In terms of an attempt. Because I am stronger than that. I might be a weak person, but I can take pain" (NME).

Six months later Detective Sergeant Stephen Morey said that, given the amount of publicity it had received and the numbers of people who would be looking for him, he assumed that Richey was "no longer with us".

It now seems sickening to think that anyone could accuse the band of cynical manipulation or using Richey's disappearance as a publicity stunt. However, at the time, such comments were rife in both the tabloid and the quality press alike. The Independent even went as far as to imply that it would increase the band's record sales, in the same way that Kurt Cobain's death benefited Nirvana's.

As the media related Richey's disappearance and self-harm to that of comedian Stephen Fry, and even Princess Diana, it was inevitable, in this period of introspection, that his behaviour would be likened to other music-related calamities. Fleetwood Mac's Jeremy Spencer went missing from his hotel in LA just before a gig. He was found later with a religious cult called The Children of God, and he refused to go back to the band. In 1970, Peter Green, also of Fleetwood Mac, gave away all of his money and disappeared. Allegedly, Killing Joke bassist, Youth, also withdrew all of his money and destroyed it in the '80s, and in March of 1982, Jaz Coleman, singer with the same band, walked out after a gig in Brighton. A couple of weeks later he was found with the Icelandic band Peyr, who, like Coleman, shared an interest in paganism.

In May of the same year, Joe Strummer walked out on The Clash just before a UK tour. When a private detective tracked him down in Paris a month later, Strummer explained that he just wanted a break. Pink Floyd's Syd Barrett left the music industry in 1968 after a period of LSD-induced mental illness. A year previously, Barrett had turned up to a show with a pot of Brylcreem mixed up with Mandrax tablets, which he poured over his head. John Lennon spent five years

from 1974-1979 cooped up in a darkened room in his apartment at the Dakota building in New York. Scott Walker vanished on the eve of an Australian tour in 1966, following a failed suicide attempt. He was found a few days later in an Isle Of Wight monastery.

Other musicians were pulled out to answer the question on everyone's lips: was Richey still alive or not? Martin Carr of the Boo Radleys told VOX he thought Richey was, Sleeper's Louise Wener thought not, and Traci Lords said, "I just hope he's OK" (VOX). Rob Stringer, managing director of Sony said:

"[Richey's] the most well-read person I've ever known – he would be able to tell you the last words of all the world's famous suicides, he would know the contents of Kurt Cobain's suicide note off by heart, and he would know 20 different ways to disappear completely. He will have planned it. He may be in Tibet for all I know" (NME).

What is it that makes mental illness so captivating? Is it the link between genius and madness, which London psychotherapist Alan Cooper describes as 'Van Gogh Syndrome'?

Cooper believes that highly creative people have a predisposition to neurosis which can lead to a detachment from reality. It's possible that insecurity makes such people seek stardom and that the affection they get in return from an audience is a kind of 'false love' which can only be detrimental to their insecurities. When Julian Cope grows his hair and wears a silly hat, he is ridiculed as insane. When Sinéad O'Connor gave away her £500,000 home after watching an appeal for Somalia on the television she was deemed deranged rather than selfless.

Writing for The Sunday Times, Cooper explained the impossible situation that Richey Edwards may have been in:

"The music industry is essentially a world where double standards apply. It is a place where two and two can make five. Contradictions are allowed. There are, on the one hand, groupies at your beck and call, and, on the other, you've got a system where you are supposed to be saint-like. Drugs and drink are easily available, and yet you're supposed to be clean-living. The internal contradictions within the system are simply mad. To disappear, to run away, to burn your money, to shun the system is often the only way pop stars can regain control of their lives."

It had been a bleak twelve months for the music world, as drugs had claimed the life of Hole bassist Kristina Pfaff and haunted the careers of Alice In Chains, Courtney Love and Evan Dando. In trying to paint a complete picture of an event that may always stay incomplete, parallels were drawn left, right and centre with other musicians. Could the eating disorder Richey suffered from be the same as Karen Carpenter's or Elton John's? Or, more morbidly, could his death be bracketed with those who had died around the same age as Richey was when he disappeared: Jimi Hendrix (28), Janis Joplin (27), Sid Vicious (21), Jim Morrison (28), Ian Curtis (23)? "He was half Ian Curtis, half Iggy Pop," Nicky told The Guardian.

With the death of Kurt Cobain (27), the analogies were inevitable. Interestingly, the music press that had covered both bands so intensely were more reserved about Richey:

"Like Cobain he is a bright, intelligent person who is also sensitive. Both were medically

"He will have planned it. He may be in Tibet, for all I know."

ill. Life in their business is not pleasant these days" (Testyn George, Western Mail).

In fact, the music-press reservation almost reached the point of self-censorship.

"We have been restrained about the whole thing in the wake of what happened with Kurt Cobain's death last year. The first time he had an overdose in Rome it was almost like a bit of sport. People felt Kurt was messing everybody about. But when he died everyone was very upset. Then when Richey disappeared everybody took it very emotionally. [We thought] Let's not make a big thing about it" (Stuart Bailie, NME).

Dr Stephen Hunter, consultant psychiatrist at Gwent Community Health Trust, said it is hard for musicians to put down roots, and therefore it's hardly surprising that they lack a sense of belonging. The incredible pressure put on musicians was recognised with the advent of Shrink Rap, a counselling organisation specifically for musicians. The late Chas Chandler, bassist with The Animals and one-time manager of Jimi Hendrix, told the Western Mail that he believed the industry attracted depressives.

In the meantime, Richey's sister, Rachel, spent much of her time on the radio, doing interviews where appropriate. "[She] wrote to every monastery she could think of, and they wrote back saying they couldn't say," Nicky told The Guardian. "So he could easily just be living a quiet life somewhere."

For some, like the conspiracy theories that continue to circulate around the deaths of Kurt Cobain and Elvis Presley, conjecture, speculation and supposition took the place of any hard evidence. Caitlin Moran wrote in The Times that she believed that Richey just wanted to escape, and that the books he had been reading about "the perfect disappearance" just added to her theory. In The Guardian, Alex Bellos remembered Richey once said that he wanted to lock himself away in a bunker like the author JD Salinger did. Simon Price, the last UK journalist to interview Richey, also still believes he is alive.

No one is comfortable with loose ends. What follows are the various rumours that have circulated in Richey's absence (the hoax calls and copy-cat incidents, of which there have been several, have not been included). None of them are by any means conclusive or exclusive. As Sherry Edwards stated, she does not believe in any of them, and as they have neither been proven or denied, they should be therefore treated accordingly.

Many of these stories mention Lori Fidler, a young American fan who had set up a Manics fanzine called Scream Tour Sigh and used to write letters, lyrics and poetry to Richey. A story ran in The Sunday Times alleging that a friend of hers had taken an overseas call and that the voice on the other end had simply said, "Hi, Lori," before hanging up. Fidler has since spoken out against The Sunday Times and bitterly denies having any knowledge of Richey's whereabouts, citing inter-fan squabbling and journalistic inaccuracies.

A pen-pal of Fidler's, David Cross, a 19-year-old student at Gwent College, from Rhigos in Abedart, believes he saw Richey just outside a newsagent by a bus station in Newport on February 5, 1995. Cross told 'Richey' that he was a friend of Fidler's. The person asked, "How is she? How's she doing?" When Cross said that she was OK, the man said, "I'll see you later," and left.

"I am positive it was Richey Edwards," Cross told VOX.

After reading about the case in the South Wales Argos, Newport taxi driver Anthony Hatherhall reported that on February 7 he had picked up a man from the King's Hotel in Newport at 7am. The passenger wanted to go to Uplands and asked whether he could lie down on the back seat. Hatherhall believed the man had a phoney cockney accent. He then asked to be taken to Risca, where he was looking for his boss who had broken down in a lorry. At this point the driver asked for some money upfront and he was given £40.

The next part of the journey was to take the unidentified man to the nearest train station. As there wasn't one very near, Hatherhall took him to Blackwood bus station, and from there onto Pontypool station, where he made a phone call. Finally he asked to go to Aust service station via "the scenic route". The bizarre journey cost £68. The Manics themselves dismissed this "mythical taxi ride that he had up the valleys" and said that it probably wasn't him because Hatherall had said that man had shoulder-length hair and Richey had shaven all his off just before.

On February 20, Mrs G Williams of Guildford said she saw a white man, around 5ft 10" tall, hitching east from Delamere services. She thought the man looked around 40 and was carrying a guitar case. When PC Garden, of Avon Police interviewed her, he faxed Harrow Road station to say

"Suggestions that he committed suicide are pure speculation."

this wasn't Richey. A week later, Anna Bowles sent a three-page theory to the NME which formulated that the star could have gone to the Holocaust anniversary being held in Germany.

During May 1995 Monika Pommer, a German fan of the band, said she had received a postcard from Richey, postmarked London and dated February 3. It said, "Thanks for all the presents, the coffee especially, take care of yourself, be happy, love Richey". A copy of a card sent to Pommer during December was sent on to the police involved in the case.

Pommer refused to send the other card, saying it was too personal and that she was carrying it with her because she saw it as a "goodbye". She proclaimed that if he didn't appear by August 20, she would travel to Cardiff and throw flowers into the sea to say goodbye.

The following month, Lucy Winters, a 16-year-old Skipton girl, said that she had seen a man, whom she believed to be Richey and described as looking "haggard and ill", carrying a tacky yellow and green rucksack. Since then, the police have been inundated with all kinds of spurious 'leads'. Bob Whitmore, of Palma Mallorca, suggested they analyse the band's lyrics and make connections to Aleister Crowley. The police said that Whitmore had misunderstood Crowley.

Missing, the LWT programme, ran an appeal for Richey in December 1995, which initiated eight calls. There were a variety of 'sightings' ranging from one in a gay pub in Brighton, to callers describing a Liverpool beggar and a busker in Cambridge. At Christmas, Richey's sister, who has spent much of her time since her brother's disappearance appealing for help and giving interviews in the hope that it may unearth new evidence, went on TV in Wales to talk about him.

Speaking of Richey's harrowing time in 1994, Sean pointed out, at the end of the band's European tour with Suede, that no one really knows what happened to Richey – "not even us". Whatever it was that made Richey Edwards such an intriguing artist may have been the same "trigger" that James later felt that his friend had no control over. The case remains open and inactive at the National Missing Persons Bureau:

"It will never close until we know exactly what happened. Suggestions he committed suicide are pure speculation. We will investigate all new evidence" (DS Stephen Moray, Press Association).

REBIRTH/AGE OF INNOCENCE

"I won't give anybody the illusion that I'm sitting th

FOR THE rest of the band, the period after Richey's disappearance was a period of suspension. Nicky spent most of his time at home in Wales, playing golf amongst other things. Sean stayed in Bristol and James hung out in London "on a demon-exorcising career as a semi-permanent... gadabout" (Dazed And Confused), being "Mr Rent-A-Party" at such haunts as The Groucho Club. Wire felt that because they had received no answers one way or another it meant that although there was still hope, the fear of finding out the worst was also still there.

"We decided to carry on in April, after two months of waiting by the phone and feeling ill and exhausted. We were really paralysed and unable to do anything. We thought we'd been so

"We thought we'd been so close, and in the end we couldn't do

close, and in the end we couldn't do anything for him. It's sad to think that perhaps he didn't like you" (Nicky, The Guardian).

"I've tried to blank it out, to a certain degree. I won't give anybody the illusion that I'm sitting there waiting, 'cos we've all nearly fucked ourselves up over it and I've developed some kind of immunity towards it. I'd rather be shocked than wait on something now. Because I can't wait around any more" (James, NME).

The month following his disappearance, the three remaining Manics met with Richey's parents and Martin Hall to discuss the possibility of continuing. Graham and Sherry Edwards raised no objections, and the band began rehearsing at the Soundspace Studios in Cardiff. By that time, James had also produced Northern Uproar's debut single, 'Rollercoaster'.

Towards the end of August 1995 the band began to put music to some of the lyrics Richey had left with them, although no comeback was definite or planned. Amid more speculation that they would disband, Sean said that it may have been on the agenda until they first practised again, in that Cardiff studio.

In retrospect, their decision to carry on does follow precedent. When AC/DC's Bon Scott died after a drinking binge, guitarist Angus Young decided that it was better to carry on working to get over the loss. They were not the only ones: The Beach Boys, Fairport Convention, Kiss, Metallica, The Pretenders, and The Band all carried on. More recently, The Charlatans decided to continue after the premature death of Rob Collins. The Manics will not be the last band to have to face the decision.

On September 4, 1995, bands from all over Britain got together and recorded a single track each to be donated to the 'Help' album, to raise money for the War Child charity and focus attention on young people caught up in the war in the former Yugoslavia. The Manics gave a live favourite to the album, a cover of Burt Bacharach's 'Raindrops Keep Falling On My Head', which they recorded at Chateau De La Rouge Motte Studio in France. Work in Bath and Abbey Road Studios followed shortly

MANIC STREET PREACHERS

REVOL
TOO COLD HERE
YOU LOVE US
(Heavenly Version)
LOVE'S SWEET

EXILE
(Bangkok Live)

afterwards. There were obviously points whilst they were recording that the band felt the loss. However, it was not particularly during studio time itself but more so in their private moments.

"The time you'd notice it was when we'd be in Nicky's room, socialising, and suddenly, there'd be a lull in the conversation and we'd all realise that that was the point Richey would have come up with one of his Richey-isms" (James, Dazed And Confused).

On December 29, 1995, The Manic Street Preachers (James, Sean and Nicky) supported The Stone Roses at Wembley Arena, making their first live appearance since Richey went missing. Rumours circulated that the Roses were worried they would be outshone by their support band, and gave them a curt soundcheck. Onstage, there was a noticeable gap where Richey would have

anything for him. It's sad to think that perhaps he didn't like you."

stood, even though John Green, an additional keyboard player (who also plays with Sleeper) had been brought in for the occasion. Between songs, the audience chanted, with remarkable insensitivity, "How's Richey?"

By the end of January the band were in Normandy, France, working on new material, using some of the lyrics which Richey had given to James just before he disappeared. Working with a

new producer, Mike Hedges (who had previously worked with Everything But The Girl, Siouxsie & The Banshees and McAlmont & Butler), the songs seemed much more uplifting – although that wouldn't be too difficult after 'The Holy Bible'. The band laid down 17 tracks.

At Sound City the band played their first headline show for 16 months at Leeds' Town & Country Club, supported by Cast and broadcast simultaneously on Radio 1. In spite of an incident in which a local woman accused James of betrayal for going on without Richey, the band saw the show as a time of "release" and described it as an "empowering" experience.

So how will they face the future? Will they be like the Stones without Brian Jones, or New Order without Ian Curtis? Their record company, Sony, described the Manics as a "top priority act" with the same potential as Led Zeppelin.

Managing Director, Rob Stringer, explains how the climate has changed:

"If the Manics were to release their debut album now, it would sell 300,000 copies. Their last record came out in September 1994, at a time when Suede were the biggest guitar act around but no one else was really doing anything big" (.dottalent/Music Week).

tle of whisky, and there was no one there."

On April 28 the group supported Oasis at their sell-out stadium gig at Maine Road. By this time the audience were chanting, "Where the fuck is Richey?" and Nicky, not surprisingly, found playing live really difficult – just "going through the motions". He described a particularly emotional point at a warm-up show at Manchester's Hacienda, where the security they had in supporting other bands had been removed:

"I remember the introduction to 'From Despair to Where', looking over to where Richey would have been standing, swigging at a bottle of whisky, and there was no one there. And when we came offstage I virtually had a breakdown, I was just crying hysterically for about three hours, like a twat. The first time I'd been able to cry since the day they found his car" (Nicky, Melody Maker).

James also said later that, when Nicky had fallen against him on stage, he had turned around to see where Richey would have been; he said he could feel the intense stare of the audience and felt that they could see his anguish. Backstage at the same gig, Sean had been talking to Peter Hook, who had said how sorry he had been to hear about Richey's disappearance. Relating it to his own experience with Ian Curtis, Hook said, "At least we had a body." Nicky told the press he was touched by this candid remark, adding that only Hook could have said it.

'A Design For Life', according to Nicky, was the most commercial track on their new album. It is also to become their biggest-selling single to date (having sold 93,000 copies in the first week). The video alone cost £80,000 to make (a mere £70,000 more than any of their others). A critique of contemporary working class culture, it was also the song that James remembers "really gave us the will to go on. As soon as I read those lyrics... I immediately remembered where I came from" (Melody Maker).

Bradfield rang up Wire just after he'd written it and told him he thought it was something special. The finished video develops the theme further, using images from their backgrounds

while adding sly references to their roots as a band with Situationist slogans such as 'A house is a machine for living in'. (The Lettrist International had damned architect Le Corbusier for designing slums –"machines for living" – and promised to build "passionate" homes instead.)

But they hadn't forgotten their old friend.

"We've also set up a trust fund so that all Richey's royalties go into this account under his name. If he ever turns up, he's got his share. That was really depressing doing all that legal shit. You've gotta wait seven years until he's declared dead. We were signing all these forms. We wanted everything to be proper, so if he ever turns up, it's all there for him. But doing that, it just makes him seem like a number. It was really sad" (Nicky, NME).

James added that it all seemed so final while they were recording 'Everything Must Go'. On the one hand, the album's success in sales terms is long overdue, but on the other, "It's tainted by the knowledge that it's not the four of us enjoying it together" (Nicky).

Sean reiterated the point by saying, "I don't care about the Number Two single. I'd much prefer it if we were still struggling and [Richey] were here now" (Select). But whenever the subject of

Richey rejoining was raised, the band drew up their guard. James, for one, doubted whether the band could pick up where they left off, because if it all happened again it would really screw him up. Nicky, however, summed up their feelings by saying:

"The album isn't a goodbye to him. We could never say goodbye. He was my best friend. We talk about him all the time between ourselves. It's easier to live with now because we're getting busy again, but you still wake up every morning and think about it" (The Guardian).

'Everything Must Go' is another rollercoaster-ride of an album. The simple cover may visibly display the three members of the Manic Street Preachers, but a fourth member is still very much featured within. Without a doubt Bradfield has a vocal clarity that is so clean compared to past material that it's hard not to assume that we should be listening hard to what is being said. Richey contributed lyrics to five of the songs (including those co-written with Nicky). These included 'Elvis Impersonator: Blackpool Pier', which questions the validity of American culture, and 'Small Black Flowers That Grow In The Sky', which was inspired after Richey had watched a programme one Christmas, about animals going mad in their cages.

Richey also penned the words to the Nirvana-Unplugged-type 'Removables', 'The Girl Who Wanted To Be God' (named after a biography of Sylvia Plath) and their third single from the album, 'Kevin Carter'. As he had often done before, Richey wanted to reclaim an artist from history's oblivion. An acclaimed photographer, Kevin Carter was chiefly known for his Pulitzer prize-winning shot of a young child dying in Rwanda with a vulture hovering close by. Carter later committed suicide, unable to deal with the pressures of fame.

Wire, often not credited for the amount of lyrics he did write, contributed striking lines about William de Kooning, the subject of 'Interiors'. De Kooning is a painter whose abstract-expressionist works of the '50s and '60s straddled the boundaries of genius and madness. The artist now has Alzheimer's disease. "We've always had a song about disease on every one of our albums," Wire told VOX, before conceding, "it's not a very good tradition to follow, really." The 'tradition' followed the likes of the machine-gun-like 'Symphony Of Tourette' from 'Gold Against The Soul', about the little-understood Tourette Syndrome, which causes uncontrollable swearing and other verbal tics.

Inevitably, the album was up for dissection, with everyone searching for hidden messages, but as always, it was the musicians themselves who really shed light on the content. "The pictures I contemplate painting would constitute a halfway state and an attempt to point out the direction of the future – without arriving there completely," reads the quote from Jackson Pollock which adorns the lyric sheet. The track 'Enola/Alone' was written after Nicky had been looking back over his wedding photographs, which included shots of Philip Hall and Richey Edwards. He couldn't help thinking how good-looking they were, and how much he missed them.

"Philip's death was so arbitrary. At least Richey exercised some kind of control, but they were both slow declines" (Nicky, Select).

Wire explained that he wrote the lyrics for 'Australia' at a point when he just wanted to run away from all the problems of the previous year, frightened that he was going to get ill himself. Wire made it as far as Torquay. But it is the album's final track, 'No Surface, All Feeling', that is their tribute to Richey. He had played the song with the band before his disappearance, and as with all the tracks, there's a real clarity in the words. Unlike some of their other material, the lyrics are very lucid; it's as if they want you to listen to what they have to say.

Once 'A Design For Life' was released, the band decided it was now time to talk about the new

MANIC STREET PREACHERS | GENERATION TERRORISTS

album and about how they had been feeling for the last year. They were completely in control of the media, once again appreciating that it was a honeymoon period: people would feel sorry for them for losing their friend on the one hand, and be probing for every emotion on the other.

"We're all glad the album's coming out when it is, I think it has a real summer side to it. We're very proud of it and I'm sure if Richey ever gets the chance to hear it, he'll feel the same," Nicky told the NME.

There was a weary air to the band; although they were undertaking yet another reincarnation of the Manics, they were also very aware of how much they had given away in the past and that everything they say is read word by word by their fans, possibly even by Richey.

Having undergone treatment for stress himself, Nicky told the press:

"I haven't got any ambition left at all any more. All that has been sucked out of me. I don't want to tour the world and change people's lives any more. I don't want to convert people to my way of thinking. All that's gone. It feels like we've given so much, and I just look back and think that maybe if we'd gone about things a different way we could all be sitting here now, healthy, happy, stable, successful people" (Melody Maker).

"I can't help thinking... Richey, if you could just have held on a little longer, things might have been a lot different. Maybe then you could have had all those things you wanted. You might have been happy" (James, Select).

The pressure on the remaining members was immense, and Nicky went on to explain, with his inimitable sense of humour, just how he felt.

"I do feel pressure to become a replacement for Richey... And I'm certainly not going to do that. We're not even going to get another guitar player in, ever... Mind you, they wouldn't exactly be queuing up for that one, would they? 'Guitar player required. Must mutilate himself on stage and carry impossible demands on shoulders forever'... All I can say is that wherever he is, whatever he's doing, I hope he's happy. Whether that's in Heaven, or in a factory in Bridlington. It would've been nice to let us know something, but if this is how it has to be, then OK. You know... I just hope he's at peace" (Melody Maker).

James also felt the pressure, with some people accusing him of being uncaring. "But what am I supposed to do?" he asked. "I loved him, and so did Nicky, and so did Sean... I can't sit in my room forever with the curtains closed being a cold fish. It's then that it's been really difficult to stop myself getting really violent" (Dazed And Confused).

Wire once again raised the New Order comparisons: both Richey and Ian Curtis had, respectively, disappeared and committed suicide on the eve of an American tour. Again, the analogies were made when journalists pointed out that the cover to 'A Design For Life' was very similar to that of 'Ceremony' by New Order, the band's first release after Ian Curtis's death.

Moving into another epoch, their fourth album was certainly more uplifting. It even included the love song they said they'd never write – 'Further Away'.

The man who had remained behind his drum kit for so much of the band's history decided that now was the time to begin talking. He had been happy for the others to take over interviews, but as he pointed out "...it's to do with the three of us, rather than the four of us now. Richey isn't in the band any more... Things will never be the same" (Select).

After tearing a ligament in his shoulder, obliging the band to use a stand-in for their performance on Jools Holland's TV show Later, Nicky and the band spent May and June of 1996 on the road, playing nine gigs at venues of around 2,000 a time. The tour was a complete sell-out. One NME journalist noted that the last time the band played as a three-piece, James had taken the weight of the band onto his shoulders and lifted it like Hercules. It was certainly true of this tour, and James held the stage impressively throughout.

During May, James guested on 808 State's new album, on a track called 'Lopez'. On July 14 they played at T In The Park, then released the title track of the album, 'Everything Must Go', as

"It's to do with the three of us now. Things will never be the same."

a single. Bradfield readily acknowledged that it stood for getting rid of some emotional baggage. On the one hand it could be taken to be about high-street bankruptcy and liquidations, but when you hear the words "And I just hope that you can forgive us, but everything must go," it becomes the "plea for understanding" that James said they were making in continuing without Richey.

"We're not saying that we've got to forget our past. Things like that will always be with you. But obviously, it is a new start in some ways. We did feel a bit free doing the album – it is such a reaction against 'The Holy Bible', musically" (Nicky, VOX).

"It doesn't mean for a second we've forgotten about Richey, but life goes on" (James, Dazed And Confused).

SEAN MOORE
Drums
All Music Cowritten with James

M s

M_SP

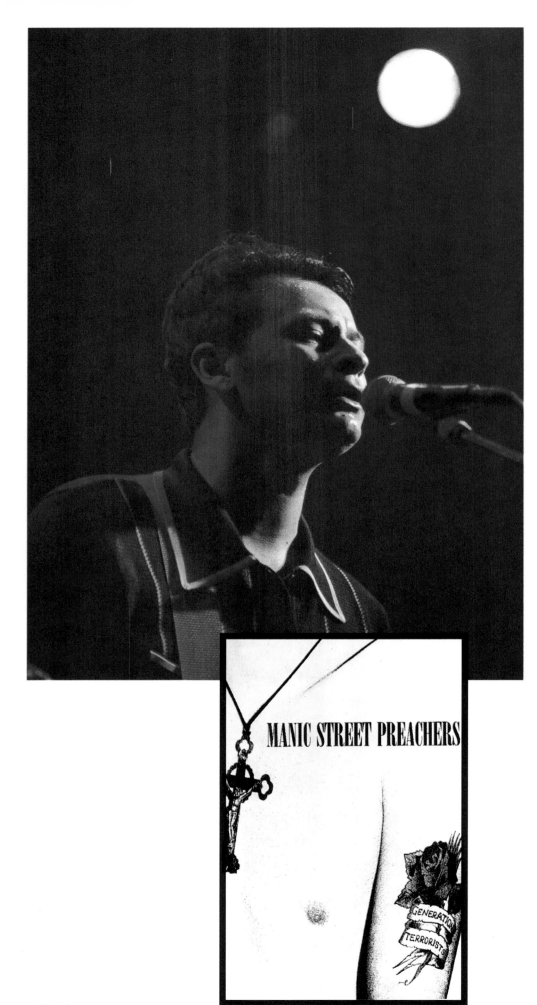

CHAPTER SEVEN

TO THE FUTURE?

"I 'VE BEEN fascinated by the Manic Street Preachers ever since I first saw them at a Heavenly Records Christmas party in December 1990: they were explosive; androgynous, disgusted, a riot of slogans, contradictions and eyeliner. If I had to describe them in one word, it would be: brave... I salute them" (Hall Or Nothing Press release, March 96, written by Jon Savage).

"I have only slipped away into the next room. Whatever we were to each other, that we are still. Call me by my old familiar name, speak to me in the easy way which you always used.

Laugh as we always laughed at the little jokes we enjoyed together. Play, smile, think of me, pray for me. Let my name be the household word that it always was. Let it be spoken without effort. Life means all that it ever meant. It is the same as it ever was; there is absolutely unbroken continuity. Why should I be out of your mind because I am out of your sight?... All is well. Nothing is past; nothing is lost... (from 'Togetherness').

In April 1992, Richey told Smash Hits that he thought they'd have drug problems and end up living in a squat in South London ("It happens to every band," he said). They had also told The Independent they would "die young and leave good-looking corpses". The Manics have been seen as the only authentic voice of alienated British youth; as class warriors and media terrorists, they have scored 14 consecutive Top 40 hits.

So what happened? Maybe Richey got the wish he expressed in '4st 7lbs', to become invisible. Who knows? The continuation of the band without its charismatic spokesman has brought the same questions that New Order faced after the suicide of Ian Curtis. Most people have applauded their bravery and simply got on with enjoying their new material. Others have been less forgiving, feeling that the band shouldn't have moved on without Richey. Nicky Wire told Melody Maker that he knew some 'cult of Richey' disciples wouldn't be happy unless everyone else in the band became ill, but he added that he just wasn't willing to fall into that trap. He has accepted the past and wants to move on, but he will not rebuke Richey for attracting such fans.

"I think connecting with those people was a positive thing, especially as no one else was giving them a voice at the time. And when your best friend was a genius, you don't want to throw away everything he stood for, just like that" (Melody Maker).

With the remainder of Richey's lyrics in their possession, the band have discussed publishing them in book form. As yet, there are no definite plans. To rejig an old quote, it's nearly the end of the millenium and the only thing that matters is the Manic Street Preachers.

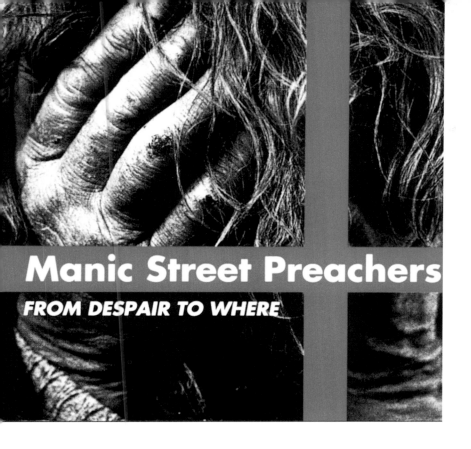

FROM DESPAIR TO WHERE

"And I hope you can forgive us, but everything must go..."

DISCOGRAPHY

ALBUMS

TITLE	TRACK LISTING	LABEL/CATALOGUE NUMBER	DATE OF RELEASE

Generation Terrorists — Columbia4710601/2/4 — 10/2/92

Slash 'N' Burn
NatWest-Barclays-Midlands-Lloyds
Born To End
Motorcycle Emptiness
You Love Us
Love's Sweet Exile
Little Baby Nothing
Repeat (Stars & Stripes)
Tennessee
Another Invented Disease
Stay Beautiful
So Dead
Repeat (UK)
Spectators of Suicide
Damn Dog
Crucifix Kiss
Methadone Pretty
Condemned To Rock'N'Roll

Also available as a double picture disc LP (5,000 copies pressed)

Gold Against The Soul — Columbia 4740649/2 — 1993

Sleepflower
From Despair To Where
La Tristesse Durera (Scream To A Sigh)
Yourself
Life Becoming A Landslide
Drug Drug Druggy
Roses In The Hospital
Notstalgic Pushead
Symphony Of Tourette
Gold Against The Soul

The Holy Bible — Epic 477421/2 — 1994

Yes
Ifwhiteamericatoldthetruthforonedayitsworldwouldfallapart
Of Walking Abortion
She Is Suffering
Archives Of Pain
Revol
4st 7lbs
Mausoleum
Faster
This Is Yesterday
Die In The Summertime
The Intense Humming Of Evil
PCP

Everything Must Go — Sony 483930/2 — 1996

Elvis Impersonator: Blackpool Pier
A Design For Life
Kevin Carter
Enola/Alone
Everything Must Go
Small Black Flowers That Grow In The Sky
The Girl Who Wanted To Be God
Removables
Australia
Interiors (Song For Willem De Kooning)
Further Away
No Surface, All Feeling

"When your best friend was a genius, you don't want to throw away everything he stood for, just like that."

DISCOGRAPHY SINGLES

TITLE TRACK	OTHER TRACKS	CATALOGUE NUMBER	LABEL	DATE OF RELEASE
Suicide Alley	Tennessee (I Feel So Low)	SBS 002		Aug 1989
New Art Riot EP	Strip It Down, Last Exit On Yesterday, Teenage 20/20	YUBB 4	Damaged Goods	22/6/90
Motown Junk	Sorrow 16, We Her Majesty's Prisoners	HVN8 12	Heavenly	21/1/91
Motown Junk (CD)	Sorrow 16, We Her Majesty's Prisoners	HVN8 CD	Heavenly	21/1/91
You Love Us	Spectators of Suicide	HVN10	Heavenly	15/5/91
You Love Us (12")	Spectators of Suicide Starlover, Strip It Down (live)	HVN12	Heavenly	May 1991
You Love Us (CD)	Spectators of Suicide Starlover, Strip It Down (live)	HVN10CD	Heavenly	May 1991
Feminine Is Beautiful	New Art Riot, Repeat After Me	CAFF 15	Caff	July 1991
Stay Beautiful	RP McMurphy	657337 6	Columbia	July 1991
Stay Beautiful (12")	RP McMurphy, Soul Contamination	657337 2	Columbia	July 1991
Stay Beautiful (CD)	R.P. McMurphy, Soul Contamination	657337 8	Columbia	July 1991
New Art Riot (EP)	Strip It Down, Last Exit On Yesterday, Teenage 20/20	YUBB 004P	Columbia	Nov 1991
New Art Riot (EP)	Strip It Down, Last Exit On Yesterday, Teenage 20/20	YUBB4CD	Columbia	Jan 1992
You Love Us	A Vision of Dead Desire	6577247 4	Columbia	16/1/92
You Love Us (Limited Gatefold 12")	A Vision of Dead Desire, It's So Easy (Live)	6577247 6	Columbia	16/1/92
You Love Us (CD)	A Vision of Dead Desire, It's So Easy (Live), We Her Majesty's Prisoners (Live)	6577247 8	Columbia	16/1/92
Slash 'N' Burn	Ain't Going Down	6578737 4	Columbia	16/3/92
Slash 'N' Burn (Limited 12" + Art Print)	Ain't Going Down, Motown Junk	6578737 6	Columbia	16/3/92
Slash 'N' Burn (Limited Gold CD)	Ain't Going Down, Motown Junk	6578737 2	Columbia	16/3/92
Motorcycle Emptiness	Bored Out Of My Mind	658037 8	Columbia	1/6/92
Motorcycle Emptiness (Limited 12" + Pic Disc)	Bored Out Of My Mind, Under My Wheels	658037 9	Columbia	1/6/92
Motorcycle Emptiness (Limited CD Fold Out Digipack)	Bored Out Of My Mind, Under My Wheels, Crucifix Kiss (Live), Under My Wheels (Live)	658037 2	Columbia	1/6/92
Theme From M*A*S*H EP	Suicide Is Painess, Everything I Do (Fatima Mansions), Sleeping With The NME	658382 2	Columbia	7/9/92
Love's Sweet Exile	Repeat	6575827 6	Columbia	28/10/92
Love's Sweet Exile (12")	Repeat, Democracy Coma	657582 2	Columbia	28/10/92
Love's Sweet Exile (Limited Gatefold 12")	Repeat, Democarcy Coma, Stay Beautiful (Live)	6575827 8	Columbia	28/10/92
Little Baby Nothing	Never Want Again	658796 7	Columbia	Jan 1994
Little Baby Nothing (CD 1)	Never Want Again, Dead Yankee Drawl, Suicide Alley	658796 2	Columbia	Jan 1994

DISCOGRAPHY SINGLES

TITLE TRACK	OTHER TRACKS	CATALOGUE NUMBER	LABEL	DATE OF RELEASE
Little Baby Nothing (CD 2)	Never Want Again, RP McMurphy (Live), Tennessee (Live), You Love Us (Live)	658796 5	Columbia	Jan 1994
From Despair To Where	Hibernation	659337 7	Columbia	June 1993
From Despair To Where (12")	Hibernation, Spectators Of Suicide (Heavenly Version)	659337 6	Columbia	June 1993
From Despair To Where (CD)	Hibernation, Spectators Of Suicide, Starlover	659337 2	Columbia	June 1993
La Tristesse Durera	Patrick Bateman	659477 2	Columbia	Jul 1993
La Tristesse Durera (Limited Posterpack 12")	Patrick Bateman, What's My Name (Live), You Love Us (Live)	659477 6	Columbia	Jul 1993
Roses In The Hospital	Us Against You, Donkeys	659727 7	Columbia	Oct 1993
Roses In The Hospital (CD)	Us Against You, Donkeys, Wrote For Luck	659727 6	Columbia	Oct 1993
Roses In The Hospital (12" Remix EP)	OG Psychovocal Mix, OG Psychomental Mix, 51 Funk Salute Mix, Fillet-O-Gang Mix, ECG Mix, Album Version	659727 7	Columbia	Oct 1993
Life Becoming A Landslide	Comfort Comes	660070 7	Columbia	Jan 1994
Life Becoming A Landslide	Comfort Comes, Are Mothers Saints	660070 6	Columbia	Jan 1994
Life Becoming A Landslide (CD)	Comfort Comes, Are Mothers Saints, Charles Windsor	660070 2	Columbia	Jan 1994
Faster	PCP	660447 7	Columbia	May 1994
Faster (10")	PCP, Sculpture of Man	660447 0	Columbia	May 1994
Faster (CD single)	PCP, Sculpture of Man, New Art Riot (in E Minor)	660447 2	Columbia	May 1994
Revol (1st CD)	Too Cold Here, You Love Us, Love's Sweet Exile	660686 2	Columbia	Aug 1994
Revol (2nd CD)	Drug Drug Druggy (Live), Roses In The Hospital (Live), You Love Us (Live)	660686 5	Columbia ·	Aug 1994
Revol (10" EP)	Too Cold Here, You Love Us, Life Becoming A Landslide (Bangkok Live)	660686 0	Columbia	Aug 1994
She Is Suffering (1st CD)	Love Torn Us Under, The Drowners (Live), Stay With Me (Live)	660895 2	Columbia	Oct 1994
She Is Suffering (2nd CD)	La Tristesse Durera (Vocal Mix), La Tristesse Durera (Dub Mix), Faster (Dub Mix)	660895 5	Columbia	Oct 1994
She Is Suffering (10" EP)	The Drowners (Live), Stay With Me (Live)	660895 0	Columbia	Oct 1994
A Design For Life (1st CD)	Mr Carbohydrate, Dead Passive, Dead Trees & Traffic Islands	663070 2	Columbia	Apr 1996
A Design For Life (2nd CD)	DFL (Stealth Sonic Orchestra Version), DFL (Stealth Sonic Orchestra Instrumental Version), Faster (Vocal Mix)	663070 5	Columbia	Apr 1996
A Design For Life (MC)	Bright Eyes (Live)	663070 6	Columbia	Apr 1996
Everything Must Go (CD single)	Block Garden, Hanging On	663468 2	Sony	July 1996

CONTACT ADDRESSES

The Samaritans - National Number   0345 90 90 90   (plus local helplines are available)
or E-Mail/Internet   Jo@Samaritans.org

The Missing Person's Helpline   0500 700 700

Bristol Crisis Service For Women   0117 925 1119
self-harm help line availalbe on Friday and saturday evenings between 9-12.30pm Also, for further information and
pamphlets on understanding self-injury write to them at: PO Box 654, Bristol BS99 1XH

The Depression Alliance   PO Box 1022, London, SE1 7QB

Childline   0800 11 11 11
(counsels people up to the age of 18, 24 hours a day)
By post at: FREEPOST 1111, London, N1 0BR

Centres Dealing with Self-Harm:
Barnes Unit, John Radcliffe Hospital, Oxford (specialists in self-harm)
Crisis Recovery, Beckenham, Kent
Offcentre has a counselling service for self harmers at 25 Hackney Grove, London

ARTICLES

NME	Barbara Ellen	Siamese Animal Men	May 28 1994
NME	Angela Lewis	Live: Anti-Nazi League Carnival	June 11 1994
NME	Ted Kessler/ Paul Moody	Live: T In The Park	Aug 6 1994
NME	News	Richey Suffering From 'Nervous Exhaustion'	Aug 6 1994
NME	News	Richey: From Despair To Care	Aug 13 1996
NME	Simon Williams	Revelation Terrorists	Aug 27 1994
NME	Keith Cameron	Don't Give Up The Deity Job	Aug 27 1994
NME	True Confessions:	Nicky Wire	Sep 1994
NME	Dele Fadele	Live: Reading	Sep 3 1994
NME	Stuart Bailie	Manic's Depressive	Oct 1 1994
NME	Caitlin Moran	Culture, Alienation, Bordeaux	Oct 8 1994
NME	Paul Moody	Live: Glasgow Barrowlands	Oct 15 1994
NME	Mark Sutherland	Live: London, Astoria	Jan 14 1995
NME	News	Manic's Richey Edwards Disappears	Feb 25 1995
NME	John Harris	From Despair To... Where?	Feb 25 1995
NME	Andy Richardson	Motorcar Emptiness	Mar 4 1995
NME	News	Richey Edwards' Disappearance	Mar 11 1995
NME	Terry Staunton	Scarpers Bizarre	Mar 18 1995
NME	News	From Despair To Everywhere	Oct 14 1995
NME	Fred Dellar	Discography	Oct 21 1995
NME	News	Richey Manic 'May Be Dead'	Nov 25 1995
NME	Stuart Bailie	Traumatic for the People	Dec 23 1995
NME	Mark Sutherland	Live: London Astoria	Jan 14 1996
NME	Stuart Bailie	Everything Must Go... On	May 11 1996
NME	News		May 18 1996
NME	Ted Kessler	Everything Must Go	May 18 1996
NME	Sylvia Patterson	Live: Wolverhampton Civic Hall	June 8 1996
Press Association	Brendan Berry	Plea to Missing Rock Star	Feb 15 1995
Press Association	Martina Devlin	Fears For Missing Rock Star	Feb 21 1995
Press Association	Jackie Burdon	Police Files Stays Open	Feb 1 1996
Q	Stuart Maconie	Smile, It Might Never Happen	Oct 1994 (?)
Rage	Damon Wise	Mild In The Country	Aug 15 1991
Raw	Paul Rees	The Manic Street Preachers	Feb 5-18 1992
Raw		Richey reviews the singles	Sep 2-15 1992
Raw	Howard Johnson	You Love Us	July 7-20 1993
Raw	Howard Johnson	Rogues Gallery: James Bradfield	Aug 18-31 1993
Raw		In The Dock: Richey Edwards	Dec 8-21 1993
Raw	Howard Johnson	Sex, Scars and Revolution	Aug 3-16 1994
Raw	Howard Johnson	Something Flipped in his Head	Sep 14-27 1994
Select	Richie Edwards	Seven Days In The Life Of...	Feb 1992
Select		Manic Porn	Sep 1994
Select	Roy Wilkinson	The Great Leap Sideways	Sep 1994
Select	Steve Lamacq	Richey Edwards In Recovery	Oct 1994
Select		A Year of Hospital Horror	Jan 1995
Select	Gina Morris	Richey Manic: Vanished	May 1995
Select	Midori Tsukagoshi	Everyone Is Weak	May 1995
Select	Stuart Maconie	We Shall Overcome	July 1996
Sky	Sylvia Patterson	Rapid Mood Swings	
Smash Hits	Sylvia Patterson	Manics Society	
Smash Hits	Dominik Diamond	The 5th Manic	
Sunday Mirror	Damian Lazarus	Last Words Riddle	April 2 1995
Sunday Telegraph	Candida Crewe	Taking It Out On Themselves	Mar 3 1993
Sunday Telegraph	Victoria McDonald	Treatment of Self-injured	Oct 29 1995
Sunday Times	Emma Forrest	Preaching to the Converted	Jan 23 1994
Sunday Times	Alex Kadis	Rocky Road	Feb 26 1995
Sunday Times	Sue Reid	The Point of No Return?	Aug 6 1995
Time Out	Peter Paphides	Cutting Edge	Dec 7/14 1994
The Times	Caitlin Moran	Preaching Revolution For Real	Dec 5 1992
The Times	Jon Savage	Oh, You Pretty Things	Apr 3 1993
The Times	David Sinclair	Drop The Attitude	Feb 1 1994
The Times	Caitlin Moran	Gorgeous In Spite of Himself	Oct 7 1994
The Times	Caitlin Moran	A Word to the Wise	Mar 3 1995
The Times	Alan Jackson	The Lost Soul	Jan 27 1996
The Times	Paul Sexton	Promises For A Golden Future	Jan 2 1996
Volume	Mandi James	Number 11	
VOX	Stephen Dalton	Dead End Street	August 1993
VOX	Bruce Dessau	Blackwood Calling	June 1991
VOX	Stephen Dalton	With A T	Sep 1994
VOX	Steve Malins	Home, James	May/June 1995
VOX	Andy Richardson	The Search For Richey Manic	Jan 1996
VOX	Paul Moody	Glam, Pain, Supernova	April 1996
VOX	Stuart Bailie	Courage Against The Machine	July 1996
VOX	Stuart Bailie	Everything Must Go	July 1996
VOX		View Art Riot	July 1996
VOX	Mark Sutherland	Everything Must Go	July 1996
Wales On Sunday	Val Bodden	Tribute To Richey	Aug 23 1995
Western Mail	Anna Morrell	Searching for the Rainbows of Life	Feb 22 1995
Western Mail	Judith Davies	Articulating the Pessimism of a Generation	Mar 31 1995
Western Mail		Missing Rock Star Was Depressed	Aug 23/271995
Western Mail	Colin Macfarlane	Rock Star's Vanishing Act	Sep 16 1995

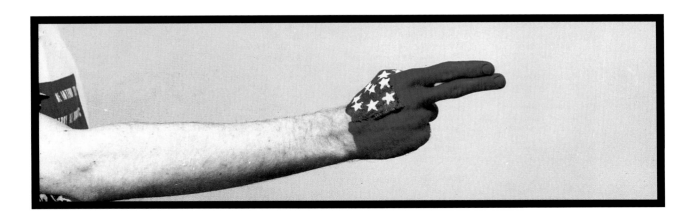

M S P

MₛP